CW0431600

Dictionary of Conversion Optimisation

An A — Z list of words and terms

With thanks to

G . F
SMITH
1885 ONWARDS

Published by Endless Gain
© Endless Gain 2016

Online sales in the UK accounted for approximately £156 billion in 2016.

While sales are up 10% year-over-year, marketing costs have also risen. In most sectors these elevated marketing costs have outpaced the growth in sales.

If this trend persists unchallenged, it will cost ecommerce businesses ever more to acquire ever less.

Continued overleaf

Owing to these unfavourable market conditions, the importance of conversion optimisation has never been greater for ecommerce businesses.

Conversion optimisation helps businesses to take back control.

By optimising their websites effectively, businesses can:
- Gain more sales
- Acquire more customers
- Reduce customer acquisition costs
- Increase revenue, *and, crucially*:
- Generate greater profits.

Furthermore, conversion optimisation can also improve the return on investment from marketing and retention channels, as visitors will arrive to a website equipped to convert them more effectively and efficiently into customers.

While conversion optimisation (CRO) has been around for nearly two decades, it has truly come into its own in the last few years as it has gained traction and developed the capacity to hold budget.

As the market matures, these budgets will increase to keep pace with the growing importance of CRO.

It is in the nature of things, now more than ever, that developments in technology tend to outpace developments in human learning. Conversion optimisation is no different.

A central challenge for ecommerce professionals is the difficulty in keeping abreast of the latest terminology, definitions, principles and practices surrounding conversion optimisation.

It is in response to this urgent need for knowledge that we have created this dictionary for you.

Putting over 1,500 words and phrases at your fingertips, the dictionary is primed to help you get through your day without feeling lost or missing an opportunity each time new jargon bubbles up in the office or elsewhere around you.

We know that this dictionary isn't something you're going to read from cover to cover, and it's not designed for that.

It's designed to be at the ready with the right info when the next unfamiliar term comes along, so that you can quickly dip in and find the answer.

We hope that our dictionary will prove to be a reliable companion on your journey to greater growth through conversion optimisation.

With kindness and best wishes,

Neil

Neil McKay
CEO, Endless Gain
neil@endlessgain.com

PS: If you ever come across any word or phrase that isn't in the dictionary but you think should be, please do let us know by emailing dictionary@endlessgain.com. If your word is added to the next edition, we'll credit its inclusion to you.

A

Aact
Attitude toward the act describes how people feel about doing something.

Aad
Attitude toward the ad describes whether we like or dislike an advert.

A/A testing
A/A testing entails split testing two identical versions of a webpage against each other. This test is used to ensure that the tool being used for the experiment is producing statistically fair results and that is no difference in conversions between the control and its cloned variation — assuming that the test is performed correctly.

Abandonment rate analysis
The purpose of abandonment rate analysis is to discover where website visitors are abandoning their shopping baskets and why they are doing it. Website analytics data will show where they are leaving the website, but some qualitative research will be needed to find out why. For example, it is necessary to discover whether the checkout process is too complicated, are there any additional, hidden costs (VAT and shipping added later), do they have to complete a long or complex registration process, are visitors being forced to create an account before they can buy, are the payment options too limited, are there any functional bugs that prevent them from continuing, and so on. Various forms of research can be used for this including surveys, chat, and eye tracking. *See also Basket recovery.*

Abilene paradox
Don't rock the boat! In an Abilene paradox a group of people collectively decide on a course of action that is counter to the preferences of many (or all) of the individuals in the group. Through conversion optimisation research, it can be demonstrated that rocking the

boat could be the best thing to do for a business; by suggesting making changes for the better based on fact not gut feeling, preferences or opinions. *(Coined by the late Jeremy B. Harvey, Professor Emeritus of Management at The George Washington University.)*

Ability
The extent to which a customer has knowledge of a product or a brand, intelligence, and the money necessary to make a purchase.

Above the fold
The area of a webpage that is visible without the need for scrolling.

SEE FIGURE 1

Absolute gaze direction heatmapping
Shows the accumulated time that test participants spent looking at the different areas of the webpage. *See also Eye tracking.*

SEE FIGURE 13

Absolute threshold
In order for a customer to detect a stimulus on a webpage there needs to be a minimal level of stimulus intensity, which is known as the absolute threshold. The threshold can be influenced by the customer's motivations and expectations, cognitive processes, and whether they have adapted to the stimulus.

A/B testing (split testing)
A/B testing compares two versions of a webpage or app — the original or control "A" and its variant "B" — against each other to determine which one performs better. During the test, incoming visitor traffic is shared between A and B. The results for both are monitored and then compared to determine whether the variant has performed well enough to select it as the new webpage or if further experimenting is necessary. When tests

include more than one variation they are referred to as A/B/n testing.

SEE FIGURE 2

Accessibility

The requirement for websites to be accessible to people with disabilities. This means that websites must cater for everyone whether they have visual, auditory, physical, speech, cognitive, and/or neurological impairments. Without catering for disabilities, a website is actively keeping its doors closed to people with disabilities. In the UK, 16 per cent of the working population have disabilities *(Disability Facts and Figures, Office for Disability Issues, UK Government 2014).*

Also, in psychological terms, accessibility is the likelihood of retrieving something from long-term memory.

Accessibility 2024

Released in 2014 by the British Columbia (BC) Government (Canada), this is a 10-year action plan that includes considerations for making the Internet accessible. Its intention is to have all BC government websites meet WCAG 2.0 Level AA compliance by the end of 2016.

Accessibility audit

The process of evaluating a website in relation to its compliance with WCAG 2.0 principles and guidelines and interaction with assistive technology to establish whether or not the site content is accessible to users with disabilities. Audits can be informal, focused on common templates that are used to build a website (such as navigation, footer, header), only concerned with the general content of the website, or detailed where a particular feature or process is reviewed. Follow up audits are generally performed once particular areas of concern have been identified and resolved.

Accessibility for Ontarians with Disabilities Act (AODA)

Applicable in Canada, the AODA came into force in 2005. It obliges businesses in Canada to make their websites accessible to WCAG 2.0 Level A between 2012–2014, and Level AA between 2016 and 2021.

Accommodation theory

How people adjust their language/communication for specific groups to gain a favourable reaction.

Acculturation

How people adapt to a new culture by acquiring skills and knowledge relevant to engaging in consumer behaviour.

AChecker

An automated online website accessibility checker that checks compliance of a website in relation to WCAG 2.0.

Acquirer (acquiring bank)

Bank or financial institution that processes card payments.

Acquisition cost

The cost of converting a new customer from various activities, including email campaigns, advertising, list rental, etc.

Acquiescence bias

The tendency for some people to agree with whatever is presented to them.

Acquisition

The process and chain of events that a customer follows to own an offering.

Action potential

An electrical signal that travels along the axon (the long, slender projection of a nerve cell), away from the cell body to the axon terminal where it triggers the release of neurotransmitters (chemical messengers).

A

Action questions
Will people click the correct link, will they find the information they need, etc.

Active space
The space between paragraphs and list items that helps with scanning (and reading where necessary). *See also Whitespace.*

Active window
The central portion of a computer screen where the bulk of the marketing copy is placed and also the area that website visitors are most inclined to focus on. It is the area where visitors should be actively engaged in the conversation process at all times.

Active voice
This is easier for people to understand than passive voice. So use instructions like *"Fill out the following form"* or *"Select one of the following options,"* etc., instead of *"The following form must be filled out"* or *"One of these options needs selecting".*

Actual identity schema
A set of multiple, salient identities that reflects who we think we are (self-concept).

Actual state
Reality — the way things really are.

Ad blocker
These prevent an Internet browser from displaying online advertisements but they also can also prevent useful Internet browsing functions.

Ad hoc research
Generally, a single research project specifically designed to address a particular problem or issue. Such research is useful when there is insufficient existing information.

Adaptation
When people get so used to particular stimuli they no longer notice them. *See also Wear out.*

Ad copy
The specific content within an advert that has the role of persuading the reader to act.

Additive difference model
Consumers compare two brands at a time by reviewing their attributes.

Address verification service (AVS)
How credit card processors verify that customers' billing addresses match the address on their credit card statements.

Adjustable text
To improve accessibility offer website visitors the opportunity to change the font size for displaying text by using a widget displayed on the homepage. This is more helpful than expecting them to go into their browser settings and make adjustments.

Adoption
The process consumers go through when they purchase and adopt a technological innovation.

Advertorial
A paid advertisement that looks like an article. They can be effective in providing useful information about a product/ service, but they must be identifiable as advertorials. Different publishers will have different rules about appearance and how they are to be labelled.

Aesthetic (hedonic) innovation
A product/service that appeals to a customer's personal taste and sensory needs. This includes user interfaces.

Aesthetic-usability effect
The tendency for people to think that an attractive product will work better than

A

a less attractive/ugly equivalent. Apple seems to have mastered this concept in the realm of consumer electronics.

Affect
To influence a customer's low level feelings/emotions.

Affect heuristic
This reflects that people make different decisions depending on how they feel. They are more likely to try new things when they feel happy, for example. Whereas, they'll be more cautious if they are unhappy.

Affect intensity
Some people will react more strongly than others to emotion-producing stimuli.

Affect referral
How people recall their feelings for a product or service, which can influence their purchasing decision.

Affective decision making
Basing a decision on feelings/emotions.

Affective function/affectivity
When feelings/emotions about a product/service influence behaviour.

Affective involvement
This requires emotional energy and initiating or heightening feelings about a product/service.

Affective responses
Feelings and images generated internally in response to a message (stimulus).

Affect-related tactics
These are based on how a customer feels about what they see.

Afferent nerves
These nerves carry all the incoming information to the central nervous system. *See also Efferent.*

Affiliate
A partner website that promotes another company's products or services and receives commission for sales or leads. If affiliated programmes are important to a business, consider analysing, testing and optimising their websites too and also optimising the landing page within a site where the affiliate traffic arrives.

Affiliate links
URLs that include affiliate identification number and additional information that makes it easier for businesses to track affiliate activity.

Affiliate programme
A performance based marketing programme set up by a company. Affiliates join the programme and are compensated based solely on their performance. Typical payment methods include a percentage of sales revenue generated or a fixed amount per specified action on the company's website.

A

Affinity diagramming
Affinity diagramming is a participatory method where concepts written on cards are sorted into related groups and sub-groups. The original intent of affinity diagramming was to help diagnose complicated problems by organising qualitative data to reveal themes associated with the problems.

Affinity marketing
Targeting buyers by their established buying patterns or trends.

Affordance
Visual clues to what an object on a webpage is supposed to do. Clearly defined CTA buttons, for example, may offer stronger affordance than using words as hyperlinks, and borders around text fields indicate that they can be/need to be filled in.

After sales
Everything that occurs after the customer has completed their purchase action, including confirmation of purchase, appropriate follow-up through exceptional fulfilment and opportunities for customers to offer feedback.

Aggregate data and metrics
This is data that are combined from several measurements that provide a summary statistic for a particular observation. This may refer to metrics such as page views, page per visit, average time on site, etc. This is in comparison with behavioural and attitudinal metrics.

Agile development
A project methodology that incorporates iteration and continuous feedback to refine and deliver a solution. It is based on empowering people to collaborate and make decisions, continuous planning, testing, integration, and other forms of continuous evolution of both the project and the solution.

AIO
The three elements to a lifestyle — activities, interests and opinions.

Ajax
Asynchronous JavaScript and XML is a set of web development techniques to create asynchronous web applications. It allows asynchronous (intermittent) data retrieval without having to reload webpages. The JavaScript element allows the application to behave like a desktop program.

Alignment
The lining up of elements to achieve balance, order, and a more logical layout. There are also four common types of typographical alignment — centre, left, right, and justified, each with its own time and place for application.

Alpha (value)
The statistical term for the significance level of a test. *See also Significance.*

Alt text
Alternative or alt text describes the nature of an image, what it is and the content. Screen readers will read the alt text so make the description meaningful. *See also Accessibility.*

Alternative-based strategy
This is when a customer makes a non-comparable choice based on an overall evaluation of what they find on a website. For example, they may dislike the options available so they make a non-comparable choice instead.

Ambiguity of information
When a consumer finds it hard to differentiate between options.

Americans with Disabilities Act (ADA)
The ADA doesn't include any specific technical requirements that it requires websites to be accessible by, but there have been instances where companies have been sued due to the inaccessibility of their websites and defendants have been required to conform to WCAG 2.0 Level A and AA.

AMP
The "Accelerated Mobile Pages" (AMP) project was announced by Google in October 2015. It is an open-source initiative for publishers to create rich content that loads quickly on mobile devices.

Amygdala (amygdalae)
The part of the brain linked to emotional reactions, notably fear and anger.

Analogous colours
Analogous colours are those positioned next to a given colour on a colour wheel. For example, red, orange, and red-orange.

These tend to harmonise with each other and are pleasing to the eye.

SEE FIGURE 3

Analysis paralysis
When people over-think their various choices and their possible outcomes when trying to make a decision. The result is that they don't make a decision.

Analysis stage
The stage of the user experience (UX) process where insights are drawn from data collecting during the earlier research stage. Capturing, organising and making inferences from the "what" can help UX designers begin to understand the "why".

Analytics
A broad term that includes a variety of tools, techniques, and processes used for extracting useful information or meaningful patterns from data. Commercially, it is about tracking the metrics that are important to the business.

Analytics audit/health check
A review of a website's analytics setup and configuration to ensure that it is collecting data accurately and appropriately to measure the website's performance.

Anchoring (focalism)
The tendency to use the first piece of information seen to inform decision making. The order of bullet points that emphasise USPs or differentiators, for example, is very important as are other visual triggers such as price reductions, comparative price plans (decoy pricing), etc.

Anchor links
Links that take website visitors to a specific place on a webpage. *See also Same page links.*

Anchor text
The clickable text in a hyperlink. *See also Hyperlinks.*

Animations
Can be helpful if used to take people through a process. But, websites shouldn't include animations just for the sake of using them. Animations interfere with peoples' tasks while they are on a website, so it is necessary to think about the relevance and usefulness of moving images, blinking text, etc., before implementing them on a website.

Animated Gif
These images have been around for 25 years and are growing in popularity. They behave like a mini video, with no sound, that can be watched from start to finish in as little as one or two seconds in a simple, auto-looping fashion.

ANOVA
Analysis of Variance (ANOVA) is used to compare the means from more than two samples (when comparing only two samples, a t-test is used). It allows the comparison of different samples at different times. *See also t-test.*

$$F = \frac{\text{between-group variability}}{\text{within-group variability}}$$

Answers
Responses to questions. For a full description of the different types of answers. *See also Created answers, Gathered answers, Slot-in answers, and Third-party answers.*

Anticipated questions
When writing web forms ensure that website visitors are asked questions they would expect to be asked. Don't surprise them with a question that appears to come out of the blue — and too early in the form. *See also Forms.*

Anxiety

Anxiety is generally the result of friction that causes visitors to question a website because of a range of problems such as complexity of forms, lack of information, problems with navigation, asking for contact information too soon, worries about security, etc. *See also Friction.*

AOI

Area of interest (AOI) defines an area within a webpage that people fixate on — for example buttons, the navigation bar, search box, links, shopping basket, etc. AOIs are set according to the research goals, and measurements typically include the time to fixation, number of fixations, fixation duration, etc. These can be analysed using eye tracking technology. *See also Fixation.*

AOV

Average order value.

API

An application programming interface (API) allows other software to communicate through an interface. An API alllows different software or programs to connect/integrate with each other.

Applet

Small add-on program that runs one specific task within the scope of a larger application. For example, a mini-software program that a Java- or Active X-enabled browser downloads and uses automatically.

Approach-approach conflict

When consumers have to choose between two or more equally desirable options. For example, choosing between holiday destinations.

Approach-avoidance conflict

This occurs when an outcome is both desirable and undesirable because it satisfies some needs but fails to satisfy others. For example, making a large purchase may fulfil some needs while at the same time it makes a sizeable loss in a person's savings or adds additional expenditure through a payment plan.

Arbitrary coherence

The initial price a visitor sees for an item on a website, even if it is a discretionary price, will influence what they think current and future prices should be.

Archetypes

Ideas and behaviours that are shared universally.

Artificiality

How experimental conditions do not reflect real-life conditions. A high degree of artificiality reduces external validity because it is difficult to project the experimental results onto the target audience.

Aspirational reference group

People who are admired and others want to emulate.

Assisted conversions

Interactions that a customer has with a website leading up to a conversion, but not the final interaction. When identifying which traffic sources convert the best, be aware that they are not telling the full story. For example, just because an organic search click was the last one before conversion, it doesn't mean it should get all the credit for converting. The visitors may have come via social media first. Therefore, it is important to optimise for a range of channels.

Assistive technologies

A range of technologies that are used by people with disabilities to access content on the web. They include magnifiers, screen readers, Braille displays — and switchers and scanners used by those with a physical disability to control input devices such as mice and keyboards.

Association cortex
The parts of brain cortex other than the cerebral cortex that assemble and interpret sensory information.

Associative reference group
The people that individuals associate with because they are seen as equals/near-equals: colleagues, neighbours, club members, etc.

ATAG 2.0
Guidelines produced by the Web Accessibility Initiative (WAI) that provide guidance for web-based authoring tool developers (such as blogs, wikis, CMS, document authoring tools, etc.) to ensure tools are accessible by people with disabilities and the content they create is WCAG 2.0 compliant.

Attention
How people allocate mental activity in response to a stimulus.

Attention driven design
Using design elements to guide and capture a website visitors' attention. *See also Clarity, White space and Visual hierarchy.*

Attention ratio
This refers to the ratio of interactive elements on a webpage to the number of campaign conversion goals. A 1:1 attention ratio means that the only action that visitors can take on a webpage is to click the call to action button or link.

Attentional bias
People generally pay more attention to something that appeals to them emotionally.

Attitude
This refers to a consumer's evaluation of a product/service — and of the website/app on which it is displayed. Attitude is based on three things: knowledge and beliefs (known as the cognitive component), feelings and emotions (known as the affective component), and behaviour (known as the conative component), which is measured in terms of the likelihood to buy.

Attitude accessibility
The ease with which a consumer remembers an attitude.

Attitude confidence
The strength of an attitude.

Attitude persistence
How long an attitude is maintained.

Attitude resistance
The level of difficulty to change an attitude.

Attitude specificity
This refers to how specific an attitude is relative to the predicted behaviour.

Attitudinal metrics
These are measures of visitor and customer attitudes towards a brand or website, etc. For example, awareness, consideration and preference.

Attraction effect
Including an inferior brand to increase the attractiveness of the dominant brand. *See also Decoy effect.*

Attractiveness
Characteristics that encourage favourable attitudes; for example, physical attraction, likeability, familiarity and similarity.

Attribute
A qualitative characteristic of a product or a service.

Attribute determinacy
Product/service attributes are classed as being salient or diagnostic, and they stimulate the brain in different ways.

Salient attributes (those things about a product that are obvious/can be seen immediately) appeal to a person's System 1 part of their brain.

Diagnostic attributes (what will this product do, what are its benefits, etc.) make people think before they take action, i.e., they trigger the System 2 part of their brain. *See also System 1 and System 2.*

Attribute processing
The process a consumer goes through when comparing available options by considering one attribute at a time.

Attribute-based strategy
Consumers make choices by comparing specific features across a range of options.

Attribution modelling
In Google Analytics, an attribution model is the rule, or set of rules, that determines how credit for sales and conversions is assigned to touch points in conversion paths. They include "Last Interaction", "Last Non-Direct Click", "Last AdWords Click", "First Interaction", "Linear", "Time Decay", and "Position Based".

Attribution theory
How we find explanations for events.

ATV
The average transaction value of a sold product or service.

Audience
This is the general target group for a site, brand or product This can be broken down to specific demographics of age, gender, profession, location, education level, interests, etc.

Audition
This refers to a person's sense of hearing and their ability to detect information from sound waves.

Audit (analytics)
A health check and review of the digital analytics set up to ensure that there is correct and reliable tracking of accurate onsite behaviour.

Augmented product
A product that adds other benefits such as service, warranty, brand reputation.

Authentication
The process of confirming a user's identity. For example, users authenticate themselves when they provide their credentials (usernames and passwords) to log into a user profile on a website. Authenticated users generally have a user profile stored in the experience.

Authorisation
Transaction performed to determine whether a payment card account has sufficient funds to complete a transaction. This may sometimes require a telephone call from the point-of-sale to obtain the authorisation. A code is generated by the card issuer (or acquirer) on approval.

Authorised retailer
An approved retailer that sells products directly to consumers.

Authority figure
A person of influence. People tend to follow the lead/advice of those they perceive as legitimate authorities (e.g., doctors, dentists, successful users of the product/service, etc.). This is particularly true when they are considering buying/ trying something new and they are uncertain about it. An authority figure can provide that reassurance.

Authority website
A website trusted by users, industry experts, other websites and search engines.

Autobiographical (episodic) memory
Knowledge people hold about themselves and their personal experiences.

Auto-complete
A feature that helps finish what a user is typing by predicting what they want to input based on previous or popular entries.

Autonomic decision
An independent purchasing decision made by either spouse.

Autonomy
People like to be in control of the situations they find themselves in, i.e., they like to do things of their own free will. Their behaviour will be influenced by how in control they feel in those situations. The more they feel in control, the less stressed they will be, and they are more intrinsically motivated to adopt the perceived behaviour.

Availability cascade
This is a theory that helps to explain the development of certain kinds of shared beliefs. It stems from the belief that if something is repeated over and over again it must be true. For example, a new or original idea (concept, or insight), that helps to explain something in a simple or straightforward manner. This is then shared among society in general — or if it is a specific idea relevant to a group, it will be shared among the members.

The idea spreads because other people have accepted it as a plausible explanation. And, it also appeals to individuals because it makes them appear that they are up to date with the idea, whether they believe in it or not. In fact, their need for social acceptance, and the obvious cleverness of the new idea, can overwhelm their ability to think critically.

Availability heuristic
Judgments made based on easy to recall past events/experiences.

Avatar
An image that represents a person when they are online.

Average gaze plotting
An average gaze plot isn't directly available from an eye tracking system. However, there is a workaround that provides a simple visualisation by calculating the average time to the first fixation on each area of interest (AOI). This visualisation only shows the order in which AOIs were fixated initially and is not an actual gaze plot. *See also AOI.*

Average order size (AOS)
Total number of items purchased divided by the total number of customer orders.

Average session duration
The total duration of all sessions calculated in seconds divided by number of sessions.

Average time on site
Metric for the average number of seconds visitors spend on a website within a specified time frame.

Average unit of sale (AUS or AS)
Total income divided by the number of customers for a particular product or service.

Avoidance-avoidance conflict
This occurs when a person has to choose between two equally undesirable options.

Awareness alerts
Website features used to gain attention. These are useful when aiming to engage with System 2. Awareness alerts use things such as disruptive visual cues to draw attention to important information, and use relevant content and/or popups that will challenge our subconscious

A

decisions, e.g.: *"Are you sure you want to cancel your subscription?"*. *See also System 1 and System 2.*

SEE FIGURE 4

Axon
The long, slender projection of a nerve cell, or neuron. The axon conducts electrical impulses away from the neuron's cell body.

Axon terminal
The end tip of an axon that makes synaptic contact with another cell to transmit information; it is the point where neurotransmitters are released.

Axure
A wireframing and interactive prototyping tool, available for both Windows and Mac.

B

Baby boomers
People born between 1946 and 1954 and coming of age in the late 1960s or early 1970s.

Back button overuse
Website visitors shouldn't need to go back all the time when they are trying to move forward through their tasks. If they do, there could be something wrong with the information architecture of the website. *See also Information architecture.*

Back end
The part of the website or web application (including the underlying database) that does not directly interact with the end user.

Back end sale
Sales made after a customer has bought their first product/service.

Back link (inbound link)
A link from one website to another.

Bait-and-switch technique
When a person is attracted by a low price but then gets enticed to upgrade their purchase to a more expensive item.

Balsamiq mockups
A wireframing and interactive prototyping tool, available for both Windows and Mac.

Bandwagon effect
How people do/believe things because numerous others do/believe the same. This helps to explain why some of the best products/services aren't selected even when they are well known to be superior. Arguably, it's like a group of friends messaging each other on Facebook instead of simply calling each other on the phone, which would be quicker and more effective. Or, people who buy a product because their peers also have it.

B

Banners
Adverts of various sizes that appear on a website.

Banner blindness
The tendency for banners to be ignored or not be seen by website visitors.

Bar graph
Suitable for graphing categorical variables that don't necessarily have any order to them. They help to emphasise the values and differences between the variables.

Bargaining
When we exchange preferences fairly.

Baseline
The starting point of a conversion optimisation experiment. For example, the baseline is the original webpage plus the data that helps to demonstrate its performance. *See also Control.*

Base rate information
Generic information collected from an activity. For example, how often an event really occurs when people use a website or an app.

Base rate neglect
Inability to calculate. Customers will, therefore, take decisions based on known numbers/percentages and ignore general statistical information. Using this to manipulate customers' behaviour, for example, being selective about customer ratings, is unethical.

Basket
This is the virtual shopping basket (shopping cart/shopping bag) that customers use when purchasing online. Items are added to the basket by clicking on a product's CTA button.

Basket recovery

Actively attempting to recover the sale once the user has abandoned the purchase process. There are various tactics available to try to win them back, including:

- Automated email sent as soon as somebody leaves the process or at a pre-determined time offering an incentive to return
- Informing the call centre to follow up to find out why the person left and try to encourage them back
- Careful use of popups or overlays offering an incentive
- It is also possible to re-market to the customer individually or group all abandoned carts together and re-market to them all. The context is important here.

SEE FIGURE 5

Bayesian

Statistical methods that assign probabilities or distributions to events or parameters based on experience or opinion of what is likely to happen before experimentation and data collection. The probabilities/distributions are then adjusted according to the results from the experiments. For example, in A/B testing, if webpage A (the control) converts at 10 per cent already, it wouldn't be expected to convert 100 per cent during the test. So, Bayesian analysis will include the 10 per cent prior knowledge into the test.

Because

Very powerful psychological word that gives justification to what has been said before it, even if what has been said after it is irrelevant "... *because* ...".

Behaviour

What people do and display in response to a stimulus.

Behavioural analytics/analysis

This is an approach that focuses on the how and why of website visitors' behaviour.

Behavioural economics

Applying insights from psychological studies to understand how and why people make buying decisions.

Behavioural intention

What people want and will do.

Behavioural metrics

These are metrics that fuel a focus on the how and why of website visitor/customer behaviour. A behavioural metric is one that actually measures a particular user behaviour, e.g., bounce rate: *"I came, I saw, I left"*.

Aggregate data may give a summary figure of average page views of 4.2 — but the behavioural metric will show the distribution of users and how many pages were viewed, and then show how many displayed a behaviour of viewing five or more pages. This can then provide segmentations that will help further understand what is happening on the website.

Other examples are things such as loyalty, recency, returning visitors, etc.

Behavioural targeting

Displaying website advertisements designed to appeal directly to visitors' specific interests and preferences. Also known as interest-based advertising, preference marketing and online profiling. Potential customers can also be re-targeted by displaying adverts in other areas of the website or on other websites that are part of the advertising network once they have interacted with the original advert.

B

Belief discrepancy

When marketing messages are different from what a person believes, resulting in counterarguments against buying the product. For example, a software program might be described as intuitive, but the person may have found it difficult to use in reality.

Bell (normal distribution) curve

Survey/sample distribution term for a graph with a large rounded peak in the middle, sloping sharply to the right and left and then tapering more gently at the extreme ends of the graph. The bell curve shows a normal distribution (or Gaussian distribution) where the vast majority of data concentrate towards the average score, with incidence of variation above and below the average being roughly equal to each other, and much less than the incidence/results towards the average and majority. *See also Gaussian distribution.*

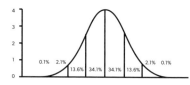

Below the fold

A concept used in user experience (UX) to indicate any information that falls under the visible area of a visitor's browser — basically, any information the visitor must scroll to see. Information above the fold generally has the highest priority because it is what a visitor sees first, requiring no interaction. *See also Above the fold.*

SEE FIGURE 1

Benchmarking

Using an existing source to compare with a similar product/service/project.

Benchmarks

As part of benchmarking, specific values of particular metrics will often be referred to as the point of comparison against which any changes achieved in optimisation will be assessed.

Benefit

The advantage attribute of a product or service.

Benefit segmentation

Segmenting potential buyers into sub-groups according to the benefits they expect from a product/service.

Best practices

Commercial or professional procedures that people recognise as being effective or the correct way to do things. In conversion optimisation, however, every website is different and so it is not possible to rely on a best practice. Instead, it is important to test and use data to find the optimal solution to improve conversions.

Beta testing (beta launch)

Tests that occur after a prototype or beta version of the experiment is complete. For example, a beta is released for a group of users who are asked to complete a series of tasks (such as log into a screen), and then data and bugs are recorded.

Bias

In research, bias is a general term referring to the inaccuracy in a study due to non-sampling errors. In consumer psychology terms, a "cognitive" bias is a systematic error in thinking that affects decisions and judgments.

Billing address

The address used for payment card bills. This can be verified using an address verification service.

B

Binary eye tracking measure

The percentage of test participants who looked at an area.

Bingo

We have a winner!

Bite-size commitment

Consumption of a product or service in small pieces. For example, downloading one song instead of a whole album.

BITV 2.0

In Germany, for web accessibility, the BITV 2.0 adopts WCAG 2.0 with some modifications and requires that all government websites comply with Level AA.

Black hat techniques

Aggressive search engine optimisation techniques that focus on getting higher rankings rather than on the website visitor. For example, keyword stacking and stuffing, using unrelated keywords, hidden links, duplicating content or mirroring a website.

Blacklist

A list of "junk" email addresses from which an email program will not accept messages. Blacklisting is one form of spam filtering.

Blog

An online journal that educates/entertains/informs and generally encourages reader feedback and drives visitors to a website.

Blocking

Emails and popups that are blocked are not processed through the ISP and are essentially prevented from reaching their addressed destination or from displaying on a customer's screen.

Bootstrapping

Self-funding a new company.

Body copy

The main part of text in a design or publication — the written website content, the book contents, it's all body copy.

Bold type

Bold type makes it easier to spot headings while scanning a webpage. Alter the size to show the various heading levels, for example page title, product, etc. *See also Legibility, Readability, and Typography.*

Bonus

Something that can be offered as an incentive to buy a product/service. It is also possible to apply deadlines and/or scarcity to the bonus too.

Boomerang technique

A technique used in moderated user testing whereby the moderator uses a generic question in order to bounce a user's comment or question back to them.

For example; User – *"Do I have to create an account?"*; Moderator – *"What do you think? / What would you normally do?".* *See also Moderated user testing.*

Bot

An Internet bot is a software application that runs scripts/automated tasks over the Internet. There are different types, for example, a web crawler (also known as a web spider or web robot) is a program or automated script that browses the World Wide Web in a methodical, automated manner to index website content. There are also spam bots that can refer fake traffic to analytics, known as referral spam. This can be tackled by setting up exclusion filters, for example.

Conversion optimisers with thorough analytics knowledge can identify where bots are at work in the analytics data.

B

Bottom of the funnel

The stage website visitors reach just before converting into customers.

Bottom up attention

Anything that makes a person look at something rather than them doing it voluntarily; i.e., bottom up attention is driven by a stimulus. A person's attention is drawn involuntarily to objects that contrast with their surroundings. *See also Top down attention.*

Bounce rate

The percentage of people who leave a website after viewing only one page.

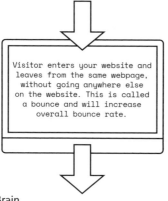

Visitor enters your website and leaves from the same webpage, without going anywhere else on the website. This is called a bounce and will increase overall bounce rate.

Brain

The part of the nervous system located inside the skull that controls thought, memory, feelings and activity.

Brainstem

The part of the central nervous system that connects the brain to the spinal cord. The brainstem contains pathways that transmit information to and from the spinal cord and peripheral nerves. It also houses the neurons that control respiration and regulate heart rhythms.

Branching factor

The total number of distinct/possible values for a discrete variable.

Brand

A collection of concepts, ideas, and emotions that encapsulate a company's values and ethos. A brand is a mix of all the fine conceptual details that make up the company, from the content the brand promotes, to the way employees talk, the words used, the values upheld, etc.

Brand alliance

When two brand names are presented together on a single product/service.

Brand association

Something or someone that makes people think about a product. In conversion optimisation, one of the objectives is to ensure that brand association is positive so that visitors convert to customers and that they ascribe trust to the website.

Brand community

A consumer group that has a structured set of relationships for a particular brand.

Brand equity

Based on customers' positive attitudes towards a brand's attributes and their use of its products/services.

Brand extension

When a company that markets a well-recognised product in a different product category using the same brand name. For example, a clothing brand extending into footwear.

Brand familiarity

When we readily recognise a brand.

Brand guidelines

A set of documented standards for rules on how to represent a business' corporate identity with visuals, text, and overall design. Guidelines often address logos, colours, typography, rules for voice and tone, and editorial conventions. For example, brand guidelines might specify

B

which logos to use and where to place each within a page.

Brand identity

The visualisation of a brand in a way that represents the values, content and ethos of the company. This can include things like a logo, business cards, letterheads, uniforms, packaging design, etc.

Brand image

How people view a brand — what they think, feel, believe, etc.

Brand loyalty

Repeat purchasing of a particular brand of product or from a specific vendor and reluctance to switch to another brand/vendor. To achieve such a strong relationship with customers requires, for example, establishing a website as their primary shopping place for those brands. There are various methods that can be used to achieve this, such as emailing them, online chats, providing excellent customer service, etc. These strategies help to reassure customers that the website shares their values and cares about their custom.

Brand personality

All of the things that reflect the image of the brand.

Brand processing

When brands are assessed one at a time.

Brand (domain) stacking

When a brand or domain achieves multiple page one listings returned by a search engine.

Breadcrumb

A type of navigation that shows the trail of pages a visitor passed through to get to the current page they are viewing.

Bricks and clicks

A business that has a physical store/office and an ecommerce enabled website.

Bricks and mortar

Businesses that have physical stores and/ or offices.

Brief

Carefully written clear instructions with background information and directions for a specific task, e.g., copywriting, website design, research project, etc. A brief can also be written for what a business expects to achieve from a marketing campaign.

Broad match

When using Google AdWords, adverts will run on relevant variations of the keywords selected by the advertiser.

Brochureware

Websites that are static in nature, provide high-level descriptive information only, and lack interactive features.

Broken code effect

Refers to unknown/unidentified bugs in a variant that are producing flawed data in an A/B or multivariate test. For example, the variant may not display correctly on some browsers and devices.

Browser

A computer program equipped with a graphical user interface (GUI) that renders and displays HTML files and used to navigate the World Wide Web. Many people may be unaware that they are using something called a browser (let alone which version they're using). To them the browser is what they use to search on the web — they don't differentiate between the browser and a search engine.

Browser compatibility

The ability of an Internet browser to properly interpret the code that makes up

B

webpages since there is slight variation between each.

Bugs

Bugs are functionality problems in a website that cause usability difficulties and stop conversions (friction) when viewed in different browsers and on different devices. All websites need cross browser and cross device testing to check for and identify bugs.

Bug-tracking system

A computer program that is intended to detect and repair programming errors.

Bullets

Used as way to list information. Bullet listed information is much easier to scan than a paragraph of text, particularly when the text contains options, a series of points, etc.

Bundling

Selling products/services as a bundle.

Business intelligence

This encompasses collecting and analysing data from various sources to produce actionable information that will aid business decisions.

Business-to-business (B2B)

Businesses that sell to each other are classed as B2B.

Business-to-consumer (B2C)

Companies that sell directly to consumers are classes as B2C.

Busy

A blanket term used to describe the design of a webpage where the visual hierarchy is not clear or is lacking. It is usually due to multiple factors such as using too many different styles and/or unclear grids.

Buy to detail rate

In Google Analytics, this is a measure of the number of products purchased per number of product-detail views.

Buyer

A website visitor who has made a commitment in principle to buy but is yet to purchase the product/service.

Buying behaviour

How someone decides whether or not to purchase a product/service. It can be influenced by various internal and external factors.

Buying process

The information gathering stage the buyer goes through before being ready to take action. Key factors for determining a person's buying process include:

- Motivation
- Fears/objections
- Questions and information sought
- The stage of the buying process; e.g., early (gathering information); middle (comparing options); or late (ready to buy).

Buying criteria

The information a person needs to answer questions, such as, *"What is it?"*, *"Why do I need it?"*, *"Why should I buy it?"*, *"How much is it?"*, etc., in order to help them make a buying decision.

Buying power

The ability to buy products/services. It is based generally on the amount of money a person has available to spend.

B

C

Caching

The process of temporarily storing HTML pages and images in a device's memory known as a cache. Caching can result in improvements in website speed.

Calculated metric (Google Analytics)

A feature of Google Analytics that allows the creation of user-defined metrics from calculations using existing metrics. These can be used to calculate bespoke metrics specifically relevant to a website that would not be available as standard, e.g., a conversion rate from any one point or goal to another. Particularly useful if also using custom metrics.

Call to action (CTA)

CTAs encourage users to act. They are displayed as buttons (primary) and text links (secondary).

To encourage a user to act a CTA must follow three clear principles:

- It must be noticed (visual hierarchy)
- It must be obvious and make sense (e.g., download your free book now)
- Users see value in taking the next step.

Call tracking (as a performance metric)

The ability to measure the number of phone calls generated from a website or advert and integrate it into digital analytics data. It is possible to measure beyond volume and also record quality, sales and volumes associated with any calls and these can be attributed back to source of generation. There are multiple methods and dedicated platforms that facilitate this ability — such as ResponseTap and Ruler Analytics, among others.

Campaign

A clearly defined, time-lined programme of marketing activities with a specific goal. The campaign's objective should be specific, measurable, achievable, realistic and timely (SMART).

Cannibalisation

Refers to a reduction in sales volume, revenue or market share of a product as a result of the introduction of a new product from the same producer. However, it can also refer to the relationship between different marketing channels or activities and sales — e.g., whether paid search takes sales that would otherwise be generated from organic search.

Canonicalisation

Individual webpages that can be loaded from multiple URLs. Having multiple URLs for the same web content can cause problems for search engines — making it difficult to determine which URL should be shown in search results.

Canonical URL

This allows search engines to be informed that certain similar URLs are the same, directing them to index a preferred URL for a particular webpage.

Cap height

In typography, the distance between the baseline and the top of capital letters.

Capital letters

AVOID USING ALL CAPITAL LETTERS IN WEBSITE BODY COPY. THE TEXT WILL LOOK UNFRIENDLY TO VISITORS, AS WELL AS SLOW DOWN THEIR SCANNING/READING. IT WILL ALSO TAKE UP MORE SPACE ON THE PAGE.

Captcha

Captcha is a program intended to protect website forms from spam entries made by bots. A/B testing has shown that removing captcha and replacing it with an alternative such as the "honey pot" technique have in some instances resulted in uplifts of 30 per cent or more. Indeed, studies have shown visual captchas can take 9.8

seconds to complete, and audio captchas can take up to 28.4 seconds, the latter having a 50 per cent dropout rate. *See also Honey pot technique.*

Card sorting

A user-experience technique using either actual cards or software, whereby participants generate an information hierarchy that can then form the basis of a website's information architecture or navigation menu.

Carpet bomb advertising

The practice of saturating potential customers with advertising on a very large scale.

Cart abandonment rate

In Google Analytics, this is the number of abandoned shopping carts (baskets) vs. completed orders.

Cart to detail rate

The number of products added per number of product-detail views shown in Google Analytics.

Categorical imperative

People place what they see into predefined categories so that they move swiftly onto the next thing. For example, if they see something like a headline on a website that is more or less identical to a headline they saw elsewhere, they will dismiss it as already seen. So, there is always a need for creativity in presenting products to visitors by using interesting, unique headlines and descriptions.

Categorisation

How people label/identify something by relating what they perceive in their external environment with what they already know.

Category listing page

A webpage for helping website visitors find what they are looking for. Also known as product listing pages.

Causal relationship

In conversion optimisation research, a causal relationship infers that two variables are related in some way (for example, warm weather causes the sale of cold drinks, ice cream, etc., to increase). Three conditions have to be met before a causal relationship can be inferred — there has to be evidence of association, the dependent variable has to change after the independent variable has changed, and all other possible causes have to be eliminated.

Causal variable

A variable that influences another dependent variable.

CDN

A content delivery network (CDN) serves static resources — CSS, JavaScript files and images. It helps to speed up a website.

CEM/CXM

Customer experience management (CEM or CXM) is how a company tracks, monitors and organises all interactions between customers and the business for the whole customer life cycle. *See also CX (customer experience).*

Central limit theorem

Regardless of the original distribution of a random variable (such as conversion rate), its average will conform to a normal "bell curve" version. *See also random variable.*

Central nervous system

The collective name for the brain and spinal cord, which can be abbreviated CNS.

Central route processing

A method of persuasion that focuses on facts and the content of a message to convince the website visitor.

Centre stage (Goldilocks) effect

People have a tendency to choose the middle option when presented with a series of choices.

C

Cerebellum

The cerebellum has two parts (hemispheres) and is located at the rear of the top part of the brain stem where the spinal cord meets the brain. It coordinates and regulates muscular activity (which is known as motor control).

Cerebral cortex

The outer layer of the brain. It is the largest and most complex part of the mammalian central nervous system and it is reportedly responsible for all forms of conscious experience, including perception, emotion, thought, and planning.

Cerebral hemispheres

The cerebral cortex is divided into two hemispheres. The left hemisphere reportedly is responsible for speech, language, writing, and calculations. The right hemisphere reportedly is responsible for spatial abilities, face recognition in vision, and some aspects of music perception and production.

C

Cerebrum

The large, highly developed, uppermost part of the human brain. It is reportedly responsible for reason, planning, memory, and sensory integration.

Challenger/champion/control

The original version of a page that is used as the benchmark against which a variation or multiple variations are measured.

Channel

The various physical means through which a website experience can be rendered, such as through desktop, smartphone, tablet, and email.

Cherry picking

When a customer is highly selective about what they buy. For example, they may only buy sale items.

Chi-square test

This test checks whether there is a difference between two or more percentages or proportions, e.g., does webpage A have more people looking at it than webpage B.

$$X^2 = \Sigma \frac{(O - E^2)}{E}$$

$X^2 =$ The test statistic

$\Sigma =$ The sum of

$O =$ Observed frequencies

$E =$ Expected frequencies

Choice architecture

The design of different ways in which choices can be presented to customers, and the impact of that presentation on their decision-making.

Choice paradox

Presenting too many options can result in fewer choices taken by website visitors, in fact they may leave without making a choice. Choice requires them to use the conscious System 2 part of their brains but this can only typically choose between about five options. *See also System 1 and System 2.*

SEE FIGURE 6

Choice tactics

We use simple rules of thumb to make low effort decisions such as when buying essential items like certain items of food, clothing, etc.

Chunking

The human ability to group larger amounts of information into related small sets, which can then be stored in short-term memory. By chunking information into smaller pieces, the functional storage capacity of the brain is increased. Therefore, information is often presented in a chunked format to facilitate human memory, for example, telephone numbers are often grouped in a xxxx-xxx-xxxx pattern.

Churn and churn rate (or attrition rate)

This is a measure of how quickly customers leave a website, which can be used to assess the impact on a business. It is also the rate (often described as a percentage) at which customers stop subscribing to a service within a given time period. It can also be calculated in revenue terms to give a financial measure of the cost to a business and the value of changes in churn rate. Particularly referenced in SaaS products.

Cialdini (Robert)

Professor of psychology and marketing (Regents' Professor Emeritus of Psychology and Marketing at Arizona State University, Phoenix, Arizona, USA) identified the six key principles of influence.

These are reciprocity, commitment and consistency, social proof, authority, liking and scarcity. He recently added a seventh principle: unity. *See also Persuasion.*

Claims

Stating something is true without backing it up with proof. It is advisable to support all claims with proof. Use customer testimonials and reviews, for example. *See also Credibility.*

Clarity

Clarity refers to both website content and design. Implemented properly, clarity will reassure website visitors that they've arrived at the right place and what they can do and why they should do it. Therefore, instead of focusing on designing a unique website, and offering cutting-edge interactive experiences, focus on the website visitors' needs for clarity so that it is easier for them to find what they want. Make things crystal clear for users.

Classic

A successful product/service with a long life cycle.

Classical conditioning

The response to a stimulus produced by repeatedly pairing it with another stimulus that produces the same response automatically.

Clickbait

Sensationalised content of limited quality that aims to attract attention and draw visitors to a particular webpage.

Click farm

Fraudulent organisations that employ low-paid workers to visit websites to post false reviews and comments or to click on PPC adverts to generate fraudulent click through advertising revenues.

Click to call

A call to action link/button that puts website visitors in direct telephone contact with sales/services/support team.

Clickability cues

A visual indication that a given word or item on a webpage is clickable. Suitable cues to indicate the clickability of an item include shape, colour, underlining, bullets, and arrows.

Clicklexia

Double-clicking on items when a single click is required, often causing the browser window or utility to open twice or ending up with duplicated items in the shopping basket.

Clicks and mortar (clicks and bricks)

Businesses that trade on the Internet as well as having traditional retail outlets.

Clickstream

A record of an Internet user, including every website and webpage they've visited, and emails sent and received.

C

C

Clickthrough (jump) page
A type of landing page that provides enough information to inform, encourage and prepare website visitors to purchase a product/service. It will contain a call to action that takes them to a shopping basket or checkout. *See also Landing page and Pathway pages.*

Clickthrough rate
This is a measure of the ratio of clicks to impressions for online adverts or email marketing campaigns. The higher the clickthrough rate (CTR), the more effective the marketing campaign is at bringing people to a website. It is measured by dividing the number of times an advert is clicked by the number of total impressions. For example, CTR = clicks ÷ impressions.

Clicktivism
Clicktivism refers to the use of social media and the Internet to advance social causes. It uses the metrics available through web analytics to optimise webpages, emails and online petitions.

Client ID
The anonymous value generated by Google Analytics (GA) to identify a browser instance and stored as part of the GA cookie.

Client-side technologies
Programming functionality that takes place in the visitor's web browser software after the landing page has been loaded. Many landing page testing changes are implemented using client-side technologies.

Cloaking
Deceptive practice of showing one set of content to search engines, while showing another to actual human visitors. When a search engine bot is identified, a server side script presents an alternative webpage. *See also Black hat techniques.*

Closing copy
The final copy written in a promotion that contains the call to action.

Cloud computing
Delivering a computing service over the Internet, which gives immediate access to hosted applications or software programs. *See also SaaS and On demand.*

Clustering
Grouping consumers by common characteristics such as what they buy, age, sex, etc., using statistical techniques.

CMS (content management system)
Software that connects to a website that allows publishing, editing and maintaining content from a central interface.

Cobranding (brand partnership)
A marketing partnership between at least two different brands of goods or services where all parties benefit from the arrangement.

Co-creation
The process where brands and consumers work together to create better ideas, products and services. For example, gathering suggestions for additional features, improvements and enhancements using user surveys.

Code freeze
An agreed period of time during which no further changes can be made to a website in order to test it.

Cognition
How people acquire knowledge and understanding by thinking and experiencing, and from interpreting information gathered using their various senses.

Cognitive age
The perceived age of a person, which may be different to their chronological age, e.g., teenagers may want to appear and

behave like they are older, while older people may try to appear/behave like younger people — in both cases, this can affect their buying behaviour.

Cognitive biases
Cognitive biases are tendencies to think in certain ways. People that think they are not affected by any bias, or think they are less biased than other people, may have a bias blind spot.

Cognitive complexity
The extent to which people prefer information to be presented to them depending on the context/task, either simply or complexly, i.e., easier tasks may require less information, while harder tasks may require more.

Cognitive dissonance
How people may feel after making a major purchase and begin to rethink what they've done when they see new alternatives. When they're in that frame of mind, they may feel that their action is inconsistent with their beliefs. So, they will try to rationalise their decision by focusing on the advantages of the product that they have bought. *See also Post decision dissonance.*

Cognitive ease/fluency
Cognitive fluency is the ease or difficulty people experience when performing a task. Their brains like to take short cuts, preferring things that are easy to think about. *See also Cognitive Strain.*

Cognitive functions
Activities and attitudes that lead to knowledge/understanding.

Cognitive involvement
The amount of information processing/ extent of importance that a consumer attaches to a product. This has a very significant effect on consumer behaviour.

Cognitive overload
A point at which too much information is provided to a website visitor for them to easily accomplish tasks, or too many tasks are provided so they can't identify the most important. Cognitive overload generally results in frustration and abandonment.

Cognitive processing difficulty
Can be caused by a wide range of things such as uncommon terminology, unclear images, complicated concepts and too much information. Eye tracking can measure the average fixation duration to gain valuable insights to the issues.

Cognitive psychology
The branch of psychology that focuses on how people process information and how they respond. In context of ecommerce, various mental processes can affect visitor experience and website performance, which ultimately can impact a website's revenue. These include, attention, memory, language, perception, problem solving, creativity and thinking. The demands placed on these processes need careful consideration when optimising a website.

Cognitive responses
Thoughts people have about a message.

Cognitive strain
Cognitive strain is affected by both level of effort and the presence of unmet demands. A person experiences cognitive strain when they struggle to read text in a poor font or faint colours, when instructions are worded in complicated language, when they cannot find answers to their questions or when the user journey is complex and unintuitive. *See also Cognitive ease/fluency.*

Cognitive (thinking) style
This describes how people think, perceive and remember information. Information can be communicated visually or verbally or by using both cognitive styles — the style can depend on cognitive ability of

C

individuals, so some people will remember what they read, others will remember an image, while others will remember what they heard.

Cohort
Group of people who share a characteristic.

Cohort analysis
Using Google Analytics, it is possible to create unique groups of website visitors that display common characteristics within a period of time.

Collaborative design
Inviting input from users, stakeholders, and other project members.

Colons on forms
Traditionally colons are placed at the end of a form label to help indicate to people using screen readers that there is a field to fill out. It is possible to use the "label" tag in the form markup instead of continuing to use colons.

Colour blind
Most people with colour blindness have an inability or a decreased ability to see red, green or blue. Colour blindness affects about 1-in-12 men and 1-in-200 women worldwide. In Britain there are about 2.7 million people (mostly male) with colour blindness. There are extremely rare cases where people cannot see any colours at all (monochromacy). *See also Accessibility.*

Colour contrast
Colour contrast can cause accessibility issues. As such, WCAG 2.0 outlines various colour contrast ratios that need to be met in order for the website to be accessible. The ratios differ depending on the level of compliance required and the size of the text being used.

Colour combinations (in forms)
Black text on a white background is a good choice. However, if the branding

requires colours, use a test pattern to highlight legibility problems. Also, consider testing colours on people with colour blindness to check whether the choices affect legibility for them.

Colour theory
The study of how colours make people feel and respond. Certain colours tend to induce particular subconscious emotions and feelings in people, for example they can make people feel safe, alert, etc. So, it is important that websites use colours that are relevant/ suitable for the target audience.

Colour wheel
The circular organisation of colour hues showing the relationships between primary, secondary, and tertiary colours.

Columbo technique
A technique used in moderated user testing, named after the American TV detective, in which the moderator is smart by acting dumb in order to coax the participant into revealing more.

One method is to ask part of a question, and trail off, rather than asking a complete thorough question. This encourages the participant to act or fill in the gaps. For example; User – *"Will clicking here add it to my basket?"*, Moderator – *"Hmmm, you're wondering if … (pause) ?".* See also *Trailing off* and *Moderated user testing*.

Common Look and Feel (CLF 2.0)
Introduced by the Government of Canada in 2011, CLF 2.0 adopts WCAG 2.0 as its website accessibility requirements and is only applicable to Government of Canada websites.

Comparative analysis
Performing an item-by-item comparison of two or more websites or apps to determine trends or patterns.

Comparative messages
Making direct comparisons with competitor brands.

Compensatory consumption
Buying something to counterbalance frustrations/difficulties.

Compensatory model
People analyse/compare costs and benefits to make a decision. For example, one particular attribute may compensate for another in assigning a preference.

Competitive advantage
Attributes that customers recognise in products/services and the accompanying service, which results in them buying from that particular brand, store or website.

Competitor analysis (also competitive intelligence)
An evaluation of the competitive landscape to determine what competitors' experiences offer. Competitive benchmarks are often used to highlight "strengths, weaknesses, opportunities and threats".

Comprehension
The process of gaining a deeper understanding about what people see by applying what they already know.

Compulsive consumption
Out of control buying. Compulsive consumers may be addicted to buying.

Computational modelling (computational marketing, computer learning)
This is the study of the behaviour of complex systems by computer simulations that produce models of behaviour. These are the ways in which automated tools will learn from users' behaviour and create and implement updates to cause a response. The technique is used for generating recommendations, suggestions for products, or content that a user may like.

Conative
How behaviour is influenced by language and attitudes.

Conceptual (cognitive) metaphor
How people make sense of a new idea by comparing it with others. Websites could, therefore, show how a product can solve a new problem by comparing it to other familiar situations that use the same solution.

Conceptual and associative priming
These are subtle cues that influence our thoughts, feelings and behaviour subconsciously.

Concept testing
Technique for exploring and testing designs early within the design phase of an experience to help identify which ideas are more effective with users than others.

Concreteness
The measure of how imaginable a stimulus or message is. Concrete stimuli are specific, and definite rather than vague and general.

Conditioning
Changing of behaviour through rewards or punishments each time an action is performed.

Cones
These are photoreceptor cells in the eye that are responsible for colour vision. They require relatively bright light to function properly. See also Rod cells.

Confidence level
The likelihood that the winning variation in a test won as a direct result of the changes made to it as opposed to just pure chance alone. Standard, is to achieve a confidence level or 95 per cent or more. Also, ensure the sample size of conversions per variation is large enough and that the test ran for full business cycle.

C

Confidence limit
The upper and lower values of a confidence interval.

Confirmation bias
A cognitive bias. The tendency for people to test things to confirm their beliefs, and cater to those preconceptions through familiarity and consistency instead of trying to alter ideas and beliefs.

Confirmation email
An automated email sent to a subscriber/ new account holder. These can contain a call to action to double-opt in or verify that they did intend signing up in the first place.

Confirmation page
A confirmation page lets website visitors/ customers know they've completed a transaction and it will inform them what will happen next.

Conformance claim
This relates to the level of conformity a website has in relation to WCAG 2.0 guidelines, whether that be Level A, AA or AAA. A conformance claim must include the date the website was judged to be conformant and the specification or standard the website is claiming to conform with and include the level of conformance.

Conformity
Following the crowd; doing what they do.

Congruence
Everything on a landing page should relate directly with a campaign goal. Incongruent elements, whether text, images, links, etc., will cause friction. *See also Campaign and Friction.*

Conjoint analysis
Determining the relative importance and appeal of different levels of a product's/ service's attributes.

Conjunctive model
A noncompensatory model that sets minimum limits for rejecting what people think are unsatisfactory/wrong options.

Conjunctive probability assessment
Estimating the likelihood that two events will occur simultaneously or that there is a relationship between attributes.

Connectedness
People will use products as symbols for their personal connections with significant people/events/experiences.

Consideration
Taking time to think about a decision.

Consideration evoked set
These are a subset of brands considered when choosing a product/service.

Consistency
Refers to uniformity of elements across a website. Providing a consistent user experience across a website is imperative because it enables visitors to quickly learn how a website operates and allows them to efficiently navigate and interact with it. Good examples are using consistent error messaging on all forms, consistent hierarchical call to action design, consistent language and consistent layouts.

Conspicuous consumption
The habit of buying and displaying products to promote personal status.

Conspicuous waste
Buying stuff that everyone can see but won't be used.

Consumer
The end user of a product/service. Note: the end user may not necessarily be the buyer of the product/service.

C

Consumer addiction

A psychological and physiological condition manifested in the need to buy products/services.

Consumer behaviour

The acquisition, consumption, and disposition of products, services, time, and ideas people make over time.

Consumer memory

The knowledge people have about products/services, shopping, and consumption.

Consumer price index

The "Consumer Price Index" (CPI) is the official measure of inflation of consumer prices in the UK. Other countries use similar indices.

Consumer satisfaction

The level of satisfaction or dissatisfaction a person feels after buying something.

Consumer socialisation

How people learn to become consumers.

Consumer to consumer

An innovative method where customers interact with each other. In consumer to consumer (C2C) markets, the business facilitates an environment where customers can sell these goods or services to each other. Online auctions as well as consumers acting as brand/product ambassadors/advocates are examples.

Consumption situation

The things other than the product or service attributes that aid the buying decision.

Contact strategy

The effort taken to better interact with customers once the company has undertaken a journey mapping effort. Usually, a segmentation has been completed using the customer data, so

that the company can be strategic in how it targets its future communications efforts.

Content

Text, images, video, sound and animations, downloadable documents, online services, email, apps, etc. In other words, everything found on a website that aims to facilitate a conversation with website visitors and help them to achieve their goals. All this information needs to be useful, accurate, up to date, credible and easy to understand.

"Written" content can be roughly divided into persuasive — the copywriting that helps people to make buying decisions — and technical — the information that helps to describe and use products/services. Conversion research will show whether the content is up to the job. *See also Copywriting and Technical writing.*

Content audit

Reviewing and cataloguing the existing repository of content.

Content brief

Outlines the vision, goals, and objectives for the content experience.

Content management

The suite of processes and technologies that support the collection, management, and publication of information. *See also CMS (content management system).*

Content marketing

Inbound marketing aimed at generating leads and traffic through distributing content that targets prospective customers.

Content matrix

A tool developed by a content strategist that documents which content will go into an experience and provides nomenclature rules. Often a content matrix is captured in a spreadsheet.

C

Content model

A tool developed by a content strategist that provides a blue print for making decisions about how, why, and when content appears within an experience. This tool is a key component in content management system design, specifying the rules for content use in wireframes and validation of visual comps (layouts of the proposed designs).

Content scraping

When a website takes content from another source and publishes it as its own.

Content strategy

The approach for figuring out which content is required for an experience. A content strategy defines the future-state content experience. It also includes the content life cycle and the governance model required to support a content experience.

C

Context

Websites are contextual. Therefore, context is important when assessing performance and objectives, etc.

Context in content

"These lightweight boots are ideal for gentle to moderate rough terrain walking" gives an immediate clue about the suitability of the boots. Setting context early in the content is very important. Don't expect website visitors to spend time searching for it, the technical description can follow.

Context of use

Demonstrate/describe precisely how the product/service would be used by real people in the real world.

Contextual effects

The influence of where a person is when they are making a decision.

Contextual interview

A form of user analysis in which a user's behaviour with a UX is examined in the context where they would use it, such as within their home. The user is interviewed as they interact with an experience. Because the user is examined within their natural environment, contextual interviews can provide detailed insight into user behaviours, wants and needs.

Continuance

Using the initial conversion to drive a second conversion request. *See also Welcome email.*

Continuity (language and writing, design)

Don't confuse customers by using different tones and styles in marketing and website copy. Also, visual elements on a landing page should match the advertising and emails to give visitors/customers confidence that they are in the right place.

Continuous experimentation

The process by which experiments are designed and iterated with the net benefit of conversion uplift.

Continuous innovation

Product/service innovations that have limited effect on consumption patterns.

Continuous variables

Variables that can take on a range of numerical values (contrast with discrete variables).

Contrast

Use contrast to promote a message in the visual hierarchy and to get people to pay attention to the message.

Control

The control page (aka champion) is the original page (A in an A/B test) that is being tested against.

Conversation

Each time a person visits a website they are trying to have a conversation with it. The website, therefore, must be able to answer their questions and inspire/encourage them to continue using it. Conversion optimisation research will discover whether a website is able to facilitate a conversation. *See also Forms.*

Conversion
The goal of a campaign.

Conversion action
A specific measurable action that is valuable to a business, such as a click to another page, form-fills, downloads or product purchases.

Conversion funnel
This describes the journey a website visitor takes as they make their way, navigating through a website on their path to making a purchase. *See also Funnel.*

Conversion metric
Measures the rate at which a user completes a task identified as a conversion.

Conversion optimisation (conversion rate optimisation)
Tuning webpages so that they make more money by changing visitors' behaviour.

Conversion optimisation process
The method used to discover how a website is leaking money and how to plug the leaks.

Conversion optimiser
A specialist who is dedicated to improving the efficiency of websites for users and businesses.

Conversion path
Step-by-step journey through a website taken by a visitor to become a customer.

Conversion rate
The percentage of visitors to complete a campaign goal.

Conversion research
Every optimisation project has to start with conversion research. It diagnoses a website and figures out where and how it's leaking money. Once this is known, the process of plugging the leaks can begin.

Conversion Research normally has three elements:

- Experienced based assessment (heuristic analysis, functionality and accessibility, usability evaluation)
- Quantitative research (web analytics analysis, eye tracking analysis, mouse tracking)
- Qualitative research (online surveys, web traffic surveys, phone interviews, live chat transcripts, customer support insight, user testing).

Cookies
Coded information that a website sends to a computer containing personal information, such as identification code, pages visited, etc., that enables the website to remember visitors at a later time. To avoid causing friction, instead of asking visitors to accept cookies, most websites have taken implied consent and made their cookie policy prominent.

Coolmining
The process of connecting with and examining youth culture to gain deeper insights into their behaviour and lifestyles.

Copy editing
Editing text for consistency and accuracy. It is a good idea to get website copy into the hands of a copy editor. They deal with the detail of grammar, spelling, punctuation, etc. Also, in certain circumstances they will fact check or highlight text for others to verify/correct. *See also Developmental editing.*

Copywriting
The art of writing persuasive content that fulfils a website visitor's information needs

C

and convinces them to take action. To do this effectively it is necessary to get inside the heads of the customers by talking to them to gain a proper understanding of the language they use. This process enables the copywriter to describe the products and services in terms that potential and existing customers understand.

Corpus callosum

Linking the right and left hemispheres of the brain is a large bundle of nerve fibres called the corpus callosum. Its job is to enable both hemispheres to share information with each other.

Correlation (versus causation)

Correlation is the statistical relationship of dependence between variables. Most often referred to when examining the dependence between two variables that have a linear relationship with one another — i.e., as one goes up (or down), so will the other — for example as traffic to a website increases so does sale volume. Be aware though that correlation does not imply causation — just because it appears that two variables change in a similar way it does not necessarily mean that one is causing the other.

Cost of goods sold

The total cost to a business for purchasing products, which are then sold to its customers. Can be abbreviated as COGS.

Cost per Acquisition

The cost of acquiring a customer.

Cost per thousand impressions

The amount to be paid by an advertiser for each thousand appearances of an advertisement on a particular webpage or set of websites.

Counterargument

When what people think disagrees with the marketing/sales message (argument).

Counterbalancing

Systematically altering the order of stimuli in A/B testing. For example, half of the test participants are shown A first and B second. The other half are shown B first followed by A. *See also A/B testing.*

Country of origin effect

How some people prefer wine from France, believe that the best cars come from German manufacturers, that Japan surpasses other countries in electronics, and so on. Their perceptions are, therefore, built on stereotypes. Websites selling products that tie into these stereotypes can exploit this effect to persuade people to buy their products.

Created answers

In form filling, created answers are those people make up there and then. *See also Gathered answers, Slot-in answers, and Third-party answers.*

Credibility

The extent to which something/someone is trustworthy, expert, or has status among a group. In the context of a website, credibility requires, for example, that:

- It looks professional
- There aren't any functionality or accessibility problems
- It has social proof and lists some high profile customers
- All copy is well written, aligned with the customer base and error free
- Displays trust and security marks
- All numbers stated are accurate — not rounded up and phrases like twice as many, etc., are avoided
- The business can prove it exists by making the "about us" page informative and include its address, photo of the building, biogs for key people, etc.

Critical incident technique

A method of gathering facts (incidents) from domain experts or less experienced users of the existing system to identify possible sources of serious user-system or interface difficulties.

Critical success factors

The criteria by which the success of an experience is determined or used within the actual product to design and build an experience. Critical success factors can translate into objectives for the experience and help the user experience project teams align a vision of what will translate to success.

CRO (conversion rate optimisation)

Whilst CRO is the term most often used to define the process of improving a website by converting more of its visitors into customers, the term CRO actually does a disservice to the process.

This is because the process of improving a website involves so much more than just optimising its conversion rate, which can easily be done without yielding any incremental growth in revenue or profit.

Terms being used more and more by industry practitioners to define the process of improving a website are 'Conversion Optimisation' and 'Growth Optimisation'.

Crowdsourcing

Crowdsourcing is the practice of engaging a "crowd", typically via social media or the Internet, to contribute to a common goal such as innovation or problem solving. Thanks to growing connectivity, it is now easier than ever for individuals to collectively contribute to a project or cause — whether with ideas, time, expertise, or funds.

CSS (cascading style sheet)

A CSS is used to set the style of a website and its pages.

Cultural probe

Cultural probes are sets of simple artefacts (such as maps, postcards, cameras, or diaries) that are given to users for them to record specific events, feelings or interactions in their usual environment, in order to get to know them and their culture. Cultural probes are used to uncover aspects of culture and human interaction like emotions, values, connections, and trust. *See also Diary study.*

Curb (kerb) cut effect

Curb (kerb) cuts are those dips in pavements that allow those in wheelchairs to get from the road and onto the path easily. It is an example of a universal design — it doesn't just apply to wheelchair users; it is also beneficial for people with pushchairs or the elderly, for example. Many accessibility (see definition) features that can be added to a website can create a curb cut effect for all users and improve access and usability.

Curiosity

A person's interest is piqued when they are presented with interesting information. They become curious and want to know more. Websites can use demos, testimonials/case studies describing how others have benefited from a product/ service to play to a visitor's curiosity.

Curtailment

Behaviour that arises from activities that use less mental energy.

Custom dimensions and metrics

Custom dimensions and metrics can be created in Google Analytics for collecting and analysing data that would not be tracked automatically. This also allows the combining of standard analytics data with customised on-site actions or values and also allows the inclusion of external data (from CRM systems, etc., or even offline activities). *See also Dimensions and Metrics.*

C

Custom reports
Analytics reports based on specifically selected metrics and data and presented in a format decided by the business.

Customer-centric
A business strategy that focuses on creating and providing a positive customer experience throughout all touch points pre- and post-sale/conversion.

Customer interactions/transactions
The way in which a customer interacts with the company's touch-points, for example, opening an email, sharing a link, or attending an event.

Customer journey mapping
A visual representation of how the organisation aligns itself to meet customer needs. It includes:

- Customer driven inbound interactions
- Company driven outbound interactions
- Interactive and face-to-face interactions
- How different interactions tie together
- Customer needs, emotions, perceptions
- The customers' expectations of their experience with the company, *and*
- Any areas where the company may be failing to meet customer expectations.

Customer lifetime value
Prediction of the net profit attributed to the entire future relationship with a customer.

Customer relationship management (CRM) system
Software that enables efficient, automated management of customer records/accounts by organising and synchronising them.

Customer retention
This is achievable through building long-term relationships with customers by gaining their trust through great service and providing an exemplary customer experience.

Customer satisfaction research
Research to gain a better understanding of how satisfied customers are with the product(s) they have bought and/or services provided by a website. Usually, this comes in the form of a survey that is filled out by the customer as close to the time of the interaction as possible.

Customer segmentation
A group of categories used to designate different types of users based on demographic and user information, such as age, purchasing behaviours, or specific socio-economic categories. *See also Baby boomers, Generation X and Millennials.*

Cut-off levels
People simplify complex choices frequently by setting attribute cut-offs. These are the minimum acceptable levels that an alternative product/service must possess to be considered further.

CVP (concurrent verbal protocol)
Used in eye tracking. Test participants think aloud by articulating their thoughts in real-time while on the task. *See also RVP (retrospective verbal protocol).*

CX (customer experience)
The various interactions the individual has with a company/brand over time. It includes the entire life cycle: awareness, consideration, purchase, repurchases, loyalty and churn. It is important to understand the customer's point of view before designing interactions and experiences that make it easy for them to accomplish their objectives.

C

D

Dark patterns
A user interface that has been designed to encourage website visitors to do things that they might not ordinarily do. They are carefully thought out and they manipulate human psychology principles, such as persuasion, to ensure their effectiveness and boost ill-gotten gains.

Dashboard (Google Analytics)
The screen that appears once logged into a website's Google Analytics. It has various widgets that can be used for an overview of the reports and metrics that interest a business. It is possible to monitor many metrics at once.

Data
Facts and statistics collected for analysis that can be used for reference. Conversion optimisation relies on data, not opinions.

Data cleansing
This involves identifying incomplete or inaccurate data and correcting them or removing them from the results. Data cleansing can result in data reduction. The process ensures data quality and prevents misinterpretation.

Data driven
An approach to activity that is based on data rather than by intuition and personal experience. The success of such an approach is very much dependent on the quality of the data collected and its analysis. Can also be referred to as evidence-based decision making or data-driven decision management.

Data duplication
Replicated customer data/records; this can create problems for the business as well as for the customer.

Data entry field
A visually well-defined location on a webpage or form where users may type data.

Data mining
This is the process of analysing large existing databases in order to discover new and useful information. Used to search for patterns in client data that indicate customer needs, preferences, and behaviours that can be used to help increase conversion.

Data quality
Effectively the suitability of the data being collected to serve its purpose in a given context.

Data sampling
A representative subset of data that is being analysed as a representative sample of a larger data set. Can be used by analytics tools in order to speed up processing time in larger data sets.

Dayparting
Describes the targeting of activity at specific times of day when it is most likely be effective with the target audience. Originally from broadcast media but also widely used in other marketing to dictate when activity is run. Important as part of any time of day analysis on conversion rates and possible impact on optimisation strategies.

Days to purchase
The number of days it takes a customer to make the decision to purchase (or other conversion). For example, see time to purchase Google Analytics report and note that it is distinguished from sessions or visits to purchase reporting.

Deadline
The final day for a particular offer. Short deadlines can encourage urgency. *See also Urgency.*

Deal prone
Consumers who are more likely to be influenced by price.

Deception

Marketing information that encourages beliefs that are incorrect.

Decision fatigue

People tend to make an automated default decision after making a lot of conscious decisions. This strategy is often seen in the gambling sector where users are encouraged to have multiple rapid micro interactions with a "game" before the macro interaction is required. Often the user makes the automated decision which often benefits the gambling website.

Decision framing

A decision requires an initial reference point or anchor.

Decision making

Selecting between options based on personal values and preferences held by the decision-maker.

Decision points

Forms that expect website visitors/ customers to decide between questions or parts of a question can cause friction. This is because they won't always read the questions, they'll simply move from field to field. For example, if a form asks for a postal code and follow on with an option to include a street, number, town, etc., the visitor sees that as the form asking for the same information twice.

Decoy effect

Also known as the "Ugly twin effect", after Dan Ariely. This can be useful for up-selling (making the higher priced item look better value than the cheapest) and for decoy selling where similar products with similar prices but different brands are available. It can be used to persuade visitors to see a specific product (or a website) as a more attractive option than the one it's being compared against.

SEE FIGURE 7

Decoy pricing

Method of pricing where the website offers at least three products, and where two of them have a similar or equal price.

Deep link

A hyperlink to a webpage with very specific information. Such a page may reside deep within a website, several links removed from the homepage.

Deep linking

Hypertext link to a page on a website other than its home page.

Demand shift behaviour

An activity that uses more efficient energy sources.

Demographics

Statistical description of a population's objective or quantifiable characteristics, e.g., age, sex, income, marital status, occupation, etc.

Dependency

When one variable influences another.

Depth of visit (average page depth)

The measure of the number of pages that a visitor views on a website. Often expressed as a distribution of the number of visits (and percentage split) at page numbers viewed. Useful when paired with measures of length of visit — as similar but distinctly different methods of understanding visitor behaviour on a website.

Descriptive statistics

The basic features of the data collected from an experiment (mean [average], median [middle value], variance [difference between an expected and actual result] and standard deviation [how spread out the numbers are]). They provide simple summaries about the sample and the measures.

D

Design control
A pre-experiment setup that aims to reduce/eliminate extraneous causal factors.

Design match
The visual design of websites/landing pages should match with the advert, email, etc., that captured the visitor's attention in the first place. If they don't match, it could cause the visitor to get anxious/annoyed and they may leave. So consistent, familiar design will help keep them on their scent trail.

Design of experiments
A systematic method for finding cause-and-effect relationships. This information is needed to manage process inputs to optimise the output. *See also Fractional factorial.*

Design research
This is research that occurs during the design process. *See also User research.*

Design stage
The stage in a user-centred design process where ideas for potential solutions are captured and refined visually, based on analysis and research performed in earlier stages of the process.

Desire
A strong wish for something. Therefore, website content should aim to encourage a visitor's wish to buy.

Determination
Using research or calculations to establish something.

Developmental editing
This type of editing comes before a website's written content is written, i.e., when the content strategy is being decided. A developmental editor can help to focus on the big picture — what to include, tone/voice, headlines, structure, etc. After the content is produced, they will look again at the content, and review whether it is achieving its goals and edit/suggest rewrites as appropriate. *See also Copy editing.*

Device analysis
Looking at user behaviour on different devices (e.g. mobile, tablet, desktop).

Diagnostic
Collecting the voice of the customer, employee and institution to understand the current state of the customer experience.

Diary study
Asking users to record their experiences and thoughts about a product or task in a journal over a set period of time.

Differential threshold
Also known as a just noticeable difference. It is the intensity difference required between two stimuli before they are perceived to be different.

Diffusion of innovation
When a new product/service is offered it will more likely be adopted by innovative people before the mass market.

Digerati
A term used for Internet and computer industry experts.

Digital analytics
A set of business and technical activities that define, create, collect, verify, or transform digital data into reporting, research, analysis, optimisations, predictions, and automations that provide insights that ultimately create business value. For example, the analysis of quantitative data collected by analytical tools from a website. This is an important part of conversion research that is necessary to drive a continual improvement of the online experience offered to customers and potential customers in order to achieve the webpage's/website's business objectives.

D

Digital journey

Understanding an individual's digital experiences with a company or brand. The digital experience should be integrated with the off-line journey, as customers usually use multiple channels to get what they need. Therefore, the digital journey only tells part of the story.

Digital native

People who have grown up with social media, smartphones and the Internet as part of their everyday lives. *See also Generation Z.*

Dilation (pupil)

Changes in the pupil indicate responses to a stimulus; but, it is not an area of interest (AOI) measure. Pupil dilation can be measured with eye tracking technology. The larger the pupil diameter, generally the higher the friction/excitement level of the website viewer. *See also AOI and Eye tracking.*

Dimensions

In Google Analytics (GA) dimensions are used to identify attributes of the data collected from a website — these are characteristics of an object that can be given different values. For example, age, gender, location, keyword, source, browser, device, and operating system are all dimensions.

The differences between a dimension and metric are:

- Dimensions are attributes of data — they describe the data
- Metrics are quantitative measurements — they measure data

In GA reports it is also possible to have "Primary" and "Secondary" dimensions. For a given report, the primary dimension is the first attribute of the data being viewed for a set of metrics. To see how those primary dimensions are further broken down, it is possible to apply a secondary dimension that subdivides the metrics for the primary dimensions by the values of the secondary dimensions.

For example, a Primary dimension may be "Source" (e.g. search, direct, organic traffic) to which a secondary dimension could be applied of "Device" category (desktop, mobile, tablet), which would show how much of each traffic source was from each device type.

In the standard GA interface reports, it is possible to combine two dimensions in this way for a given report view, hence Primary and Secondary. And, by using other tools (Query Explorer or the Reporting API) it is possible to pull reports that have a breakdown by multiple dimensions in one report.

Diminishing returns

The point at which the level of profits or benefits from a particular activity decrease – diminish – regardless of how much money or other resource is invested in the activity.

Direct response copywriting

Copy written to elicit an immediate response using a call to action, such as landing pages for newsletter subscriptions, sales webpages, etc. *See Indirect response copywriting.*

Direct traffic

This is traffic reported in Google Analytics where Google cannot identify any information showing where the visitor has arrived from. Generally, this is the traffic from visitors who will have entered a website URL directly into the browser address bar (or possibly have bookmarked the website in previous historic visits). This is often viewed as a mark of how much awareness there is of a website but it can be inflated due to tracking issues in the GA set up when the identifying information

D

has been lost or is unavailable to GA for some reason. *See also Analytics audits.*

Directional cues

Visual elements on a webpage that are intended to guide website visitors' attention to call to actions, for example. There are explicit directional cues such as arrows and/or lines, people pointing, etc., or suggestive cues that utilise colour, contrast, white space, etc.

Directories

Websites that list and link to other websites.

Disability Discrimination Act of 1992

In Australia, the DDA 1992 section 24 makes it unlawful for a person who provides goods, facilities or services to discriminate on the grounds of disability. It is supported by the World Wide Web Access: Disability Discrimination Act Advisory Notes created by The Australian Human Rights and Equal Opportunity Commission (HREOC), and although there is no legal requirement to follow these advisory notes they provide guidance on how to avoid discriminatory practices when developing web content. The notes are based on WCAG 2.0.

Disconfirmation

The discrepancy between what people expect from a product/service and its actual performance.

Discontinuous innovation

A game changing/disruptive product or service that solves an existing problem in a new way.

Discounts

These can take a number of forms that may encourage people to buy, e.g. price cuts, reductions on multiple purchases, lower cost shipping, etc. Care is needed when applying discounts and special offers because they can backfire. Instead,

customers should purchase from a website because they want to (intrinsic motivation), not because they feel compelled to take advantage of a one-time offer (extrinsic motivation).

Discovery of what matters

Knowing what needs optimising and where. This is critical for conversion optimisation. Discovery of what matters is through data collection, testing, and analysis.

Discrete variables

A discrete variable must take a certain value from a finite set (while continuous variables can take any value, e.g., time).

Discursive processing

How the brain processes images as words.

Disjunctive model

This is a consumer attitude formation model. According to the model, people have minimal satisfaction standards about a product's features that are most important to them. It allows them to ignore what they think are unimportant features while considering/making a purchasing decision.

Disruptive

A design or idea that changes the market. Airbnb and Uber are commonly cited as examples.

Dissociative reference group

The people that others don't want to follow or aspire to being like.

Distraction

Anything that stops the user from achieving their intended goal. The "law of distraction" highlights that System 2 (see definition for System 1 and System 2) cannot manage more than one decision at a time. So, they have to put full attention to one task at a time. For the website visitor, simplicity is, therefore,

D

very important. This can be achieved by removing distractions on the webpage. Too many distractions on a website could postpone decisions. *See also Clarity, Dual process theory, and Friction.*

Distributor
A business that supplies and sells products from a number of manufacturers to retailers. They may offer shorter lead times and the ability to buy in smaller quantities than a manufacturer.

Diversification bias
When people choose multiple things for future consumption simultaneously, they tend to select a variety. This tendency to diversify is less likely when they make sequential decisions.

Diversity
Just like bricks and mortar stores, a website needs to cater for and reflect the diversity of its visitors/customers.

Doctrine of foreseeability
Vendors are obliged to anticipate situations in which their products can be misused, and to warn the buyers or users accordingly.

DOCTYPE
The <!DOCTYPE> declaration is an instruction to the web browser about what version of HTML the webpage is written in. It is not a HTML tag.

Dogmatism
The resistance to change, new ideas and/or innovations.

Domain name
The address of a website (for example, endlessgain.com). It is used in URLs to identify particular webpages.

Domain specific values
Values that apply to only a particular area of activity, e.g., health, religion, family, sport, etc.

Door in the face technique
A persuasive technique to encourage compliance by making a very large demand, followed by a smaller demand that the person deems more reasonable.

Dopamine
This is a neurotransmitter that helps to control the brain's reward and pleasure centres (and is also associated with pain). It also helps to regulate movement and emotional responses, thereby encouraging us to move towards the reward or what will give us pleasure. *See also Reward system.*

Drop down label/menu
A graphical control/navigational element that allows website visitors to select one value from a list and enable information capture. For example, quantity of a product. If there are too many options, however, a drop down list can become a usability issue. Test before implementing.

SEE FIGURE 8

Drop ship
An arrangement between a retailer and a supplier to ship products direct to the buyer. This can be done strategically because the retailer purposely doesn't hold the stock or tactically because supplies have run out, which can help with overcoming problems with back ordering.

Dual coding
When a person's memory recognises a stimulus as images and words.

Dual process theory
The human brain has two modes of thought (a dual process): fast, instinctive and emotional "System 1" (implicit), and

D

slower, deliberative and logical "System 2" (explicit). Websites have to be able to activate both systems to be effective. *See also System 1 and System 2.*

Duplicate transactions
An error in analytics tracking whereby the same transaction is recorded more than once and is skewing data for conversion rate and volume. Generally discovered in an analytics audit phase using a duplicate transaction report to identify multiple instances of the same unique order ID being recorded in the data.

Dynamic content
Website content that changes to suit the visitor/customer. The content adapts according to previous purchases, location, etc., which makes offers less generic. Dynamic content, therefore, makes the user experience more personal.

D

Early adopter
A person who starts using a product or technology as soon as it becomes available.

Earned status
Status acquired through achievement.

Echoic memory
People remember what they see and hear very briefly.

Echoing technique
A technique used in moderated user testing in which the moderator repeats the last phrase or word the user said, while using a slight questioning tone, in order to encourage the user to elaborate on what they said without leading them.

For example, User – "This form is odd", Moderator – "The form is odd?". *See also Parrot technique and Moderated user testing.*

Ecological validity
This requires that the methods, materials and setting of a study must approximate the real-world.

Ecommerce
The business of online retailing. It entails selling products/services online on desktop, tablet and mobile devices via individual websites, marketplaces like Amazon and eBay, and other channels such as app stores.

Ecommerce tracking
The process of capturing and reporting online transactional data.

EEG
An electroencephalogram (EEG) is a device used to measure and record electrical activity in the brain. It can be used to monitor/measure responses to stimuli for consumer psychology purposes.

Efferent
This refers to outgoing information or a neuronal connection that sends information out of the central nervous system.

Ego depletion
Ego depletion (sometimes called ego fatigue) refers to when a person's energy level for mental activity is low. This impairs their ability to focus conscious effort (System 2) on making a decision, which makes them more susceptible to persuasive tactics. *See also System 1 and System 2.*

Eisenberg Hierarchy of Conversion
A conversion optimisation theory that explains that when people visit a website, they enter at the bottom of a pyramid of needs. When the base needs at the bottom of the pyramid are met, potential customers can move up to address the next need. So, a website must function properly on all devices and browsers, it must be accessible to all visitors, and every visitor must be able to use it, which allows an intuitive experience. And finally, if all the other layers of the pyramid are dealt with successfully, the website must provide a persuasive value proposition.

SEE FIGURE 9

Elaboration
How we transfer information into our long-term memory by processing it at deeper levels.

Elaboration Likelihood Model (ELM)
This psychological model aims to explain different ways of processing stimuli, why they are used, and their outcomes on attitude change. It proposes two major routes to persuasion: the central route (now known as System 2) and the peripheral route (now known as System 1).

SEE FIGURE 10

E

The peripheral route is used when the person has little or no interest in the subject and/or has a lesser ability to process the message, while the central route is used when the person has the motivation as well as the ability to think about the message and its topic. It suggests that if motivation is high, then deep processing is possible by the central route. *See also System 1 and System 2.*

Email marketing
A powerful marketing communication method for directing people to a website.

Email service provider (ESP)
An online tool for managing email distribution to managed lists of subscribers, e.g., MailChimp.

Embedded links
Hyperlinks included in text. Careful use is necessary as they can be distracting and may take people away from the core information they should be reading. So, consider the context in which they are used.

Embedded markets
Markets where the social relationships among buyers and sellers change how they operate.

Emblematic function
Products used as membership symbols by social groups. Emblematic function can be wide ranging and is contextual, for example, wearing a badge, a logo, owning a particular brand of product, and so on.

Emotion
The way a person feels about other people, brands, products, etc., will manifest in some form of emotional response. Emotions can affect any interaction and they may change from the beginning of an interaction to its end. An angry customer being treated fairly and respectfully by a customer service representative could turn their emotional state from angry to satisfied, or even delight.

Emotional appeals
Messages/arguments designed to get emotional responses.

Emotional arousal
This includes fear, anger, curiosity, love, and so on. These emotions may be felt with overpowering intensity that results in an action and can be manifested by facial expressions and pupil dilation. For example, when a visitor is aroused by what they see on a website, their pupils may dilate. This can be monitored/measured using an eye tracking system.

Empathy
Understanding what other people feel and desire. To ensure a website and what it offers is relevant to the visitors, it is necessary to understand them and to think like they do. Various surveying and research techniques can help to establish empathy.

Emphasis framing
This persuasion technique focuses on particular aspects of a product/service that encourage people to interpret them in a certain way, and in doing so they avoid focusing on the other aspects.

Encapsulation
Using boxes, colour, shading, etc., to make things stand out on webpages. *See also Attention.*

Encoding of evidence
How we process information from our experiences.

Endowment effect
Placing greater value on the things that a person owns, rather than on what they don't own or would like to own. Also known as ownership bias and divestiture aversion.

E

Enduring involvement
Extended interest in something that has been bought, or an ongoing interest in a product.

Engaging or engagement
Capturing the user's attention or interest or maintaining their interaction.

Enhanced ecommerce tracking (Google Analytics)
The advanced set up of ecommerce tracking in Google Analytics that enables the capture of additional data on site and provides a host of additional powerful reporting features.

Equality Act 2010
In force in the UK, this act does not specify how accessibility should be implemented but requires those that sell or provide services to the public to not discriminate against any person requiring the service or product.

Equity theory
This can be applied to the fairness of an exchange (or exchanges) between a buyer and seller, which helps in understanding customer satisfaction and dissatisfaction. For example, if a customer believes that a product/service is priced fairly, or even a bargain, then their satisfaction will be high.

Equivalence framing
This persuasive approach seeks to present certain information in a way to encourage particular interpretations while discouraging others. Opposite terms are often used in equivalence framing. For example, people will be influenced by gains rather than losses, whether something is full rather than empty, whether a certain food contains fat or is fat-free, and so on.

Ergonomics
In relation to a website, this is its ability to respond effectively and easily to the needs

of visitors/customers, and provide them with a comfortable user experience while they are browsing, filling in forms, etc. *See also Human factor.*

Error bars
Error bars represent the variability of data and are used on graphs to indicate the error, or uncertainty in a reported measurement. They give a general idea of how precise a measurement is or how far from the reported value the true (error free) value might be. They can be represented graphically or as a numeric plus or minus range around the average or mean observed value.

Error message
An on screen message that signals that there is a problem with an instruction from a website visitor's device or there may be a fault with their hardware/software or there is a fault with the website itself. The error message should explain why the error occurred and what will happen next, whether it is something that the website visitor is expected to do to take them to the next step (e.g. go to another webpage) or if it's something that needs fixing on the website. It should offer reassurance to prevent annoyance/anxiety.

Escalation
This refers to the need to move a website visitor's query, complaint, etc., further up the chain of responsibility. For example, visitors/customers cannot find the answers to their questions in a help section or anywhere else on the website. Therefore, it is helpful to include a dedicated email address and/or telephone number so that they may contact one of the team for a personal answer. *See also Trust.*

Estimations of likelihood
How likely something will happen.

E

Ethical hacking

Penetrating a computer system or network to find security vulnerabilities. Ethical hackers aim to answer whether the website is secure enough to trust with users' data.

Ethics

An individual's or group's moral principles that direct/govern right and wrong behaviour.

Ethnography/ethnographic research

The process of gathering information about users and tasks directly from users in their normal work, home or leisure environment. Ethnography focuses on long-term studies spanning weeks, months, or even years. Information may be collected through participant observation, interviews, audio or video recording, observer logs, artefact collection, diaries and photographs. *See also Contextual inquiry and Culture.*

Evaluative criteria

The measures people use to help decide between competing products/services.

Event

Events are a method of tracking user interactions on site in addition to a standard webpage view or a screen load. Downloads, filter and sort use, gadgets, button clicks, AJAX embedded elements, and video plays are all examples of actions that can be tracked as events.

In Google Analytics there are three levels of naming for events, category, action and label which allow you to construct a powerful framework for reporting all user interactions on your website.

Evoked set

The options people identify as being able to satisfy their needs.

Evolutionary design

Evolutionary design is a process of taking what is known to work on a website and retaining those features/functions while making incremental improvements or redesigns to the other areas that don't work as they should.

Exact match

Exact match refers to using Google AdWords and choosing to show an advert to customers who are searching for an exact keyword (or close variants of an exact keyword). *See also Broad match.*

Exit pages

Where visitors leave a website.

Exit popup

An on screen message that displays automatically (usually in a box format) at the point when a visitor leaves a website.

Exit rate

Not to be confused with bounce rate. Exit rate looks at the number of people leaving from any individual page, regardless of how many pages they visited earlier.

Expectancy disconfirmation model

This psychological model attempts to explain a person's tendency to form a belief about a product/service because of their prior experience with it, or having learnt about it from other sources. Their belief is usually based on their expectancy about the quality of the offering.

Expectancy value model

This model explains how attitudes form and change over time. For example, once a person has bought a product, their perception of it may alter the longer they own it.

Expectation

This refers to what visitors/customers want from a website. For example, they may expect fast and engaging web

E

experiences. Conversion optimisation research is the optimal way to find out their expectations and how they can be met.

Experience architecture
Multidisciplinary approach to technology involving information architecture, interaction design and experience design practices that aim to provide a good user experience and, therefore, benefit business.

Experience map
A holistic, visual representation of a website visitors' interactions with an organisation when zoomed right out (usually captured on a large canvas).

Experience models
A graphical representation that captures how a user envisions a system. Experience models are used to represent how a user thinks about an experience and their engagement with it.

Experimental studies
These are practical research studies where an intentionally introduced treatment, procedure, or program is observed, recorded and reported.

Experimentation
Is the act of conducting a controlled test or investigation.

Experiments
Experiments test existing theories or new hypotheses to support or disprove them. They provide insight into cause and effect by demonstrating the outcomes when a particular factor is manipulated.

Explicit memory
Memory of a prior episode accessed through actively trying to remember.

Explicit motives
The conscious drivers that motivate a website visitor/customer to complete an action. These originate often from the belief of the individual and their desire for reward.

Exponential diffusion curve
This explains how when a product comes to market there is a rapid growth in sales (adoption of the product) for an initial short period, which then levels off over time. Sales can continue, but they are at a slower rate.

Exposure
The process by how we make physical contact with a stimulus.

Exposure to evidence
The actual experience of a product or a service.

Expressiveness function
The use of products as symbols to stand out from others.

Extended Parallel Process Model
This psychological model attempts to predict how individuals will react when confronted by fear-inducing stimuli. It is commonly used in encouraging people to adopt a healthy behaviour, e.g., quit smoking, eat more fruit and vegetables, get screened for a disease, etc. For fear-based campaigns to be effective, they must induce a moderately-high level of fear and a higher level of self-efficacy and response-efficacy. If the level of fear is too high or not high enough, the message is ineffective.

SEE FIGURE 11

External search
How people collect information from outside sources such as search engines, magazines, advertisements, brochures, etc.

E

External validity
The extent that measured causal relationships in an experiment can be applied to uninvolved people.

Extremeness aversion
This refers to alternatives where the middle option is seen as the least extreme. When comparison shopping, for example, if a person sees three items that appear identical, they are more likely to choose the mid-range priced option.

Extrinsic motivation
Doing something because some external factor — a person, an organisation, bank balance — is exerting an influence over the person. *See also Intrinsic motivation.*

Eye
A specialised organ that reacts to light and enables vision. The lens focuses on an object and the retina captures the image, resulting in chemical and electrical events that send nerve impulses to the brain's visual cortex through the optic nerve. *See also Foveal vision.*

SEE FIGURE 12

E

Eye tracker
Technology that measures the position and movement of eyes.

Eye tracking
Measuring the gaze point of a website viewer's eyes or the movement of their eyes relative to their head in real time. The technique is accurate and uses specialist equipment to provide a wealth of data that supports other essential conversion research.

SEE FIGURE 13

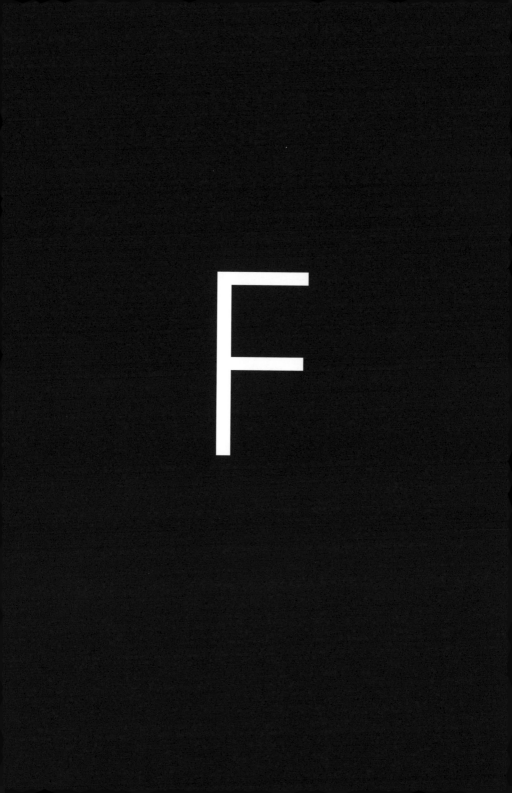

Facebook

Facebook is a popular, free social networking website that allows registered users to create profiles, upload photos and video, send messages and keep in touch with friends, family and colleagues.

Facial distraction

The brain is programmed from an early age to scan faces. In doing so, people can miss other persuasive information on website product pages because they are distracted by focusing on the face of a model, for example.

SEE FIGURE 14

Facilitator

A person who leads a discussion or activity to extract feedback and information. For example, they may want to develop an understanding of a situation or an objective, help achieve consensus among a group, understand the differences or obstacles that stand in the way of end goals, and clarify various points of view. Their skills include timekeeping, applying behavioural tools to help achieve the desired test or activity goals, listening, asking questions, suggesting alternatives, and moving the test or activity forward and record keeping. They may also chair various forms of user research.

Facts

Information that should reflect the truth about something. Stating facts in website copy can be persuasive, but always check their accuracy. Use respected sources/authorities.

Failed test

Where the variant/s didn't beat the control in a test. Even a failed test should produce learning.

Fallacy

A misleading or false belief.

False accuracy (precision)

A misleading statistic due to missing detail. It occurs when data are presented in a manner that implies better precision than is actually the case. For example, 0.78 and 0.7899 represent different probabilities.

False bottom

Horizontal lines or spaces on a webpage that make the visitor think they've reached the end.

False-consensus effect bias

A bias displayed by people who assume that their own beliefs/opinions/values reflect those of society. In the context of a website, for example, everyone hates carousels, everyone closes popups without reading them, and so on.

False positives

Test results that indicate that something is present when it is not.

FAQs

Frequently asked questions (FAQs) are asked directly by visitors and customers of a website — or should be. They should not be questions and answers developed internally by the business without input from the people that use the website. They can be very valuable if they provide real information and they are not used as marketing pitches. Useful FAQs respond to the questions that the customer services and technical support teams receive, and should be updated regularly. However, there is a school of thought that the website content itself should be able to pre-empt any questions arising by containing all the necessary detail to explain products, services, delivery and returns policies, etc.

Favourability

How much a person likes/dislikes something.

Fear appeal

A message or an argument that stresses negative consequences. It is a

F

persuasive message that aims to arouse fear presenting a risk and the vulnerability of the person to the risk. The message may or may not suggest a form of protective action. Danger signs and insurance sales techniques use fear appeal.

Feature phones
Mobile phones without touchscreens, but have interactive features such as Internet connectivity, email, txt messaging, the ability to store and play music, etc.

Feedback
Information used for modifying the process that produced it.

Feedback loop
Information transmitted backwards to an earlier part of the neural pathway.

Feed-forward network
This refers to when a signal from one point in a neural pathway is transmitted forward, thereby adding information to the circuit.

Felt involvement
How people feel in response to a stimulus. For example, they may display interest, excitement, anxiety, passion, and engagement, depending on the context.

Fidelity
The level of detail of the test stimulus. Low-fidelity stimuli include sketches and wireframes, while high-fidelity stimuli are more like a finished product in terms of behaviour and appearance.

Figure and ground
How people interpret stimuli in the context of a background (Gestalt psychology). This is vital for recognising objects using eyesight, such as recognising words on a page. The figure could be interpreted as two faces looking towards each other with a white background or a chalice in front of a black background.

SEE FIGURE 15

Filters
Functional features that make it possible to control/refine the data provided by an analytics platform. And, they do a similar job on websites, allowing visitors to filter through a list of products by selecting different attributes.

First click attribution
An attribution model that gives credit for a sale/conversion to the first click that drove a user to the website irrespective of any subsequent visits driven by other sources. *See also Attribution models.*

First impression task
A usability test to determine whether people recognise the intention of a website/webpage. Test participants are given a scenario to establish context before they see the website/webpage that they'll be asked to use. After a few seconds of looking at it, they will establish their goal and try to interact with it.

First-party cookie
A cookie set by the particular internet domain or website that an internet user is visiting. *See also Cookies.*

Fitts (Paul)
Psychologist and an eye tracking pioneer. In 1947, for the purpose of improving aviation safety, Fitts and his fellow researchers used cameras to study the movement of pilots' eyes as they used their cockpit controls and instruments to land their aircraft.

Fitts' law
This suggests that the further away a target is, and the smaller its size, the longer it will take for a user to reach it. The time required to move from a starting point to within the confines of a target area is dependent on a logarithmic relationship between the

distance from the point to the target area and the size of the target.

Five second test
Quick usability test in which a user is shown a page of a website (or application) for five seconds and then asked questions about what they recall. Can be used to gauge the clarity of webpage designs.

Fixation
When the eye stops to look at something. Fixations last from less than 100 milliseconds to half a second. Reading fixations last for about 200 to 250 milliseconds, while scene viewing fixations can be longer, 280 to 330 milliseconds. Fixations are measured using eye tracking.

Flat design
This is the trend of using clean, uncluttered interface design. However, it is important not to forget about affordance — i.e., sufficient visual clues that something can be done when a website visitor clicks on a button, for example.

Flicker effect
When a website visitor sees the original (control) page for a fraction of a second before they see the test variation.

Floating headings
These are headings that appear too far away from the related content. They can be confusing to website visitors who may not immediately recognise that the floating heading is referring to the following text, for example. Fix the problem in the website's cascading style sheet (CSS).

Flow reports
Google Analytics reports that visualise user journeys through a website. There are multiple similar reports that are focused on different elements including user, behaviour, goal, event and social user.

Fluid layout
When a page contracts and expands horizontally inside a person's web browser despite the size of the browser window or the resolution of the monitor.

fMRI
Functional magnetic resonance imaging (fMRI) is used to measure brain activity by detecting variations in blood flow through the brain. For example, changes in blood flow can indicate excitement or friction at seeing a particular product image.

Focus group
A group discussion where a moderator leads a group of participants through a set of questions on a particular topic. Focus groups are often used in the early stages of product planning and requirements gathering to obtain feedback about users, products, concepts, prototypes, tasks, strategies, and environments. Focus groups, however, have limitations when it comes to websites and apps. One or two people can influence the group with their ideas, so they don't present their own personal views. And, focus groups are discussion groups; they are not hands on website users.

Focus map
A simplified version of a heat map showing visually less attended zones.

Focusing effect
An effect that occurs when a person places emphasis on the importance of one thing at the expense of others. Generally, people can only do one thing at a time. Their System 2 part of the brain, therefore, requires a low number of easily comparable choices. This is important when highlighting unique selling points (USPs) — and the most important USP should be highlighted to encourage greater attention.

F

Fogg behaviour model

Behaviour = motivation + ability + trigger, or B = mat. All of those elements must happen at the "same moment" to elicit the behaviour. *See also Yerkes-Dodson Law, which describes correlation between arousal and performance.*

SEE FIGURE 16

Fold

The area of a webpage that divides what can be seen when first looking at the page with what can't be seen because it is beneath the "fold", and requires the user to scroll. *See also Above the fold.*

SEE FIGURE 1

Fonts

Text characters that have a specific style and size. For many years, serif fonts (**A, a, B, b, C, c**, etc.) have been the norm in print. However, on the web the general tendency is to use sans serif fonts. Consequently, people have become familiar with sans serif fonts.

It is advisable to select a legible, familiar sans serif font as the default (e.g., Verdana, Arial, Helvetica). It ought to be one that is common to most computers and devices to ensure that the text is rendered properly. *See also Legibility, Readability and Typography.*

Foot-in-the-door

A persuasive technique where an individual is asked to agree to a small request, which opens up opportunities to ask them to agree to further, bigger requests later. The technique can help build trust between a buyer and a seller.

Footer

The bottom of a page or template. Footers generally include information and navigation elements that are less important than main navigation items, but still important, such as privacy policies of a company.

Forced choices

A psychophysical method that is designed to elicit a response by making it necessary to select an option. For example, opt out rather than opt in; Do you want next day delivery? Yes, or No; and so on.

Forced device jumping (keyboard/mouse switching)

Unnecessarily forcing users to change input devices to complete tasks.

Form analytics

Tools designed to highlight friction on forms — they help to identify the fields that cause problems for users.

Formatting text

Refers to the treatment and organisation of text. Because website visitors scan websites to find what they are looking for, it is important to format text to make it easier for them to get the information they want. Good formatting uses useful informative headings, short paragraphs — bulleted lists, and key terms are highlighted in bold. *See also Readability.*

Formative research

This is used to develop effective strategies to influence behaviour change. Formative research identifies and enables an understanding of the characteristics of target audiences (e.g., their interests, behaviours) that influence their decisions and their actions. As such, formative research is integral to developing conversion optimisation programs as well as improving existing conversion optimisation projects.

Form elements (controls)

Input elements like text fields, check boxes, radio-buttons, submit buttons, select lists, text area, field set, legend, and label elements.

F

Form label alignment

Refers to how labels (instructions/ questions), that indicate what information is required, are aligned on a form. Label alignments typically are at the top, right, left or inside the form field itself.

Top aligned labels (labels placed above the form fields) appear to work better than other alignments because users aren't forced to look separately at the label and the input field. They only require a single eye fixation to take in both input label and field. *See also Forms and Labels.*

Form optimisation

Improving the conversion opportunities for web forms. Badly designed forms with poor interaction will encourage potential customers to leave a website before they've done what they need to do. Form optimisation includes:

- Informing the visitor what the form is about
- Simplifying the task by asking only for the information really needed
- Using a single column and avoiding multi-column layouts
- Labelling form inputs to decrease the cognitive load (the total amount of mental effort needed) on the user
- Using a progress indicator on long forms.

Forms are linked to final conversions on most websites. Therefore, optimising a website's forms can help to increase conversion rates and profits.

Forms

Interactive data collection mechanisms that enable customers to input contact details, product choices, etc. They should be thought of as the way that a website converses with visitors/customers. Forms need to be easy to complete and must not raise anxieties for the visitor or they may leave the website before completing a purchase, for example. Layout, microcopy, and error messaging can influence whether a website visitor will complete a form.

Fovea

The fovea is a small, central pit composed of closely packed cones in the eye and is responsible for sharp central vision. *See also Eye and Foveal vision.*

Foveal vision

This is just 1° of a person's entire 180° field of vision beyond direct line of sight, which is processed by the fovea in each eye. To get an idea of the coverage, hold an arm out straight and look at the thumbnail — when people look at a website that is the total area of what they will see in fine detail. This has implications for the positioning of webpage elements. *See also Eye and Fovea.*

SEE FIGURE 17

F-pattern

How people are thought to view webpages. The F-pattern was the discovery of Jakob Nielsen, Nielsen Norman Group.

SEE FIGURE 18

However, contemporary studies show things have changed. For example, eye tracking studies show that with the development of Search Engine Results Pages, incorporating rich text and adverts, people now look all over the page.

Fractional factorial design

Experimental designs that use a carefully chosen fraction or subset of the experimental runs of a full factorial design. *See also Full factorial, Main effect and Variable interactions.*

Frames

Obsolete method that was used in designing websites. Frames were used to simplify maintenance of shared content,

F

but they created usability and accessibility problems. CSS, server-side includes, PHP, CMS, dynamic HTML, Ajax, etc., have superseded frames.

Framing
This is a cognitive bias. People frame things (ideas, opinions, etc.) either positively or negatively. On a website it is possible to encourage positive framing by highlighting testimonials, focusing on the benefits of a product/service, explaining the benefit of monthly payment plans for large purchases, etc. *See also Gain-Framed Language and Loss-Framed Language.*

Fraudulent symbols
Objects, logos, emblems, etc., that lose their status/validity because of widespread adoption for other purposes than what they were originally designed to do.

Frequency and recency
The number of visits to a website, how many page views, how frequently visitors return, and how recently those visits have occurred. Frequency is, in effect, the count of the number of instances, while recency is a measure of time.

Frequency heuristic
Beliefs based on the number of supporting arguments and/or how many times those arguments are repeated.

Frequentist
Researchers that use probability to model sampling. They draw conclusions from sample data by emphasising the frequency or proportion of the data.

Friction
Friction is a general term for features on a website that cause problems for visitors/customers. The effect of friction is to slow down or stop website visitors from becoming customers or existing

customers from doing what they want to do. It can be caused by many variables such as design, poor copywriting, copy and graphics that look like they are interactive but aren't, placement of webpage elements, how many steps it takes to complete a purchase, the amount of information customers are expected to provide, unclear instructions, etc.

But sometimes friction is a good thing. If a website removes friction on a form field it may get a lot of leads but these leads may be of poor quality. Adding friction in may reduce the volume of the leads but increase the quality.

Frictionless checkout
The experience of checking out without any problems.

Front end
Refers to client-side development of HTML, CSS and JavaScript for a website or web application.

Frontal lobe
One of the four major lobes of the cerebral cortex in the mammalian brain, which is located at the front. It is reportedly involved in attention, decision making, abstract thinking, evaluating/problem solving, emotion, intellect, muscle movements, smell, personality, and directing behaviour. It contains most of the dopamine-sensitive neurons in the cerebral cortex.

FUD
Refers to a website visitor's fear, uncertainty, and doubt about products, services or whether they are on the right website.

Fudge factor
This is a theory that dishonesty is commonplace among all people and, therefore, we all have the capacity to cheat and lie about 10–15 per cent of the time. Individuals will do this so long as they are able to have a positive view of themselves.

Fulfilment
Refers to warehousing, stock management and delivery, generally outsourced to a third-party to save on cost.

Full factorial multivariate test

In this type of test the traffic is spread evenly across all variations. This multiplies the amount of traffic needed for statistical significance.

Functionality and accessibility
Each element of a website must function properly and must be accessible by all visitors on all required devices and browser versions.

Functional needs
People look for products/services to solve their consumption-related problems (needs).

Funnel
A funnel helps with visualising and comprehending the customer journey through a website before finally converting to a sale. Funnel describes the decrease in numbers that occurs at each step of the process, thereby indicating areas for optimising.

SEE FIGURE 19

F

G

Gain-framed language

Language can be gain-framed (quit smoking and live longer) or loss-framed (smoking kills). Both of these approaches can be tested to see which has maximum impact with the target audience. *See also Loss-framed language and Framing.*

Galvanic Skin Response (GSR)

Also known as skin conductance or electro-dermal activity it is a marker for emotional arousal, usually measured by the output of secretion from sweat glands and levels of conductance in the skin. The higher the emotional stimulation/arousal the higher the skin conductance.

Gamification

Using gaming style approaches to engage and retain customers through rewarding them for their actions. Loyalty programmes, where points are awarded for making purchases and referring friends/family, are examples.

Garbage in, garbage out

Phrase used in computer science, mathematics, and conversion optimisation and abbreviated as GIGO, which describes the concept that the quality of the output is determined by the quality of the input. In conversion optimisation, this may refer to performing poor (or not doing enough) research leading to poor hypothesising and testing.

Gatekeeping

Controlling the flow of information.

Gateway

Refers to an ecommerce service that authorises credit and debit card payments for online purchases. *See also Payment gateway.*

Gathered answers

In form filling, customers may be expected to gather answers from various places: credit/debit cards, their computers, physical files, etc. It is a good idea to let them know in the form introduction that they will need to provide certain information rather than partway through filling it out. *See also Slot-in answers, Third-party answers, and Created answers.*

Gaussian distribution

A data distribution also known as a bell curve. *See also Bell curve.*

Gaze cueing

We automatically focus our attention on what others are looking at.

Gaze placement

We only notice what we're gazing at.

Gaze plot

Shows a test participant's fixations as dots, and saccades as lines. The size of the dots represents the length of fixation — so the bigger the dot, the longer the fixation. The number of dots and their sizes seen in a gaze plot is dependent on the parameters of the test. *See also Eye tracking.*

SEE FIGURE 13

Gaze replay

Replaying a gaze pattern recording to a test participant. It is used as a memory cue but does not provide perfect recall of the test. These need to be used carefully (if at all) as they can affect subsequent tests because they make test participants aware of their gaze behaviour.

Gaze video

Dynamic visualisation of a test participant's point of gaze as they look at a webpage. Depending on the system, the gaze is shown as a moving dot or a crosshair.

Gender

Gender refers to characteristics that pertain and differentiate masculinity and femininity. Depending on the context of how gender is being used, these

G

characteristics could include biological sex (male, female or intersex), sex-based social structures (e.g., gender roles and other social roles), or gender identity.

Generation X
People born between 1965 and 1976 coming of age in the late 1980s and early 1990s.

Generation Y
People born between 1977–94 coming of age around the Millennium. *See also Millennials.*

Generation Z
The group of people born around the Millennium and coming of age from 2013 onwards. They are seen as the first generation of true digital natives.

Geofencing
A technique that allows marketing messages to be sent to mobile devices when they enter a specified location.

Geotargeting
Delivering content to a potential customer/existing customer relative and relevant to their location.

Gestalt principles
People do not visually perceive items in isolation, but as part of a larger whole. These principles include human tendencies towards similarity, proximity, continuity, and closure.

Gestalt psychology
Gestalt psychology sees objects and scenes in their simplest forms — because of this, it is sometimes referred to as the law of simplicity. The theory proposes that the whole of an object or scene is more important than its individual parts, making it impossible to deduce the attributes of a whole object from analysing its parts by themselves. Therefore, the object or scene is interpreted as a "pattern"

or a "configuration." For example, the configuration of the black shapes in the logo of the World Wildlife Fund enable us to interpret the patterns as a giant panda.

Global elements
Page links or functions of a website or application that are present throughout.

Global navigation
A means to access primary content or functions from every page.

Global values
Our most enduring, strongly held, and abstract values (that hold in many situations).

Goal conversion rate
The percentage of visits to a website where the visitors achieve their goals.

Goal derived category
Things that we put in the same category because they serve the same goals.

Goal directed attention
When a person is able to focus their attention on key tasks or goal, i.e., they are initiating the attention. It is not being directed by an external stimulus as in stimulus-driven attention. It is a System 2 behaviour and is also known as "top down" attention/behaviour. See also Stimulus-driven attention, System 1 and System 2, and Top down attention.

Goals
In conversion optimisation testing, a task's goal will influence how a test

participant views a website/webpage. Goals need to be realistic to emulate what would happen in a real-world website visitor situation.

Also used in Google Analytics as the name for conversion tracking that is not based on ecommerce tracking.

In psychology, goals represent future behaviour or behavioural outcomes that usually result in a positive difference.

Google Analytics

Google's site analytics solutions. Now compromises a suite of products under the banners of Google Analytics (Free), GA premium and GA 360 Suite.

Google Analytics 360 Suite is the latest iteration of the product that incorporates all the main individual products including the below:

- Adometry by Google — a Google purchase ad attribution company develop to give marketing attribution and optimisation insights
- Tag Manager — site container tag management platform
- Data Studio — data visualisation and reporting tool
- Audience Center — data management platform (DMP) used to collect and organize customer data
- Big Query — managed cloud based data warehouse for processing and interacting with very large data sets
- Optimise — Google's site testing and personalisation platform.

Google Keyword Planner

An online tool designed to help select the most effective keywords for advertising campaigns.

Google Search Console

This is free service from Google that helps monitor and maintain a website's presence in Google Search results. Search Console can help webmasters understand how Google views the website and to optimise its performance in search results.

Google Trends

An online search engine tool that informs how often a particular term or keyword is searched for on Google. It can be used for comparing keywords or phrases. It shows where searches came from and how search volume has changed over time.

Graceful degradation

Website functionality that provides a certain level of user experience in more modern web browsers, that degrades gracefully to a lower level of user experience in older web browsers.

Graph

Enables information to be processed in parallel, making it easier to understand test results, etc. See Line graphs, Bar graphs and Pie graphs.

Graphical user interface (GUI)

See User interface.

Grey (unofficial) market

Trading products through distribution channels that are legal but unintended by the original manufacturer.

Grid

Framework made up of evenly divided, intersecting columns and rows. Grids help designers to align and arrange elements in a quicker, neater, and more consistent way.

Groundhog Day

The movie, starring Bill Murray, represents the purest form of A/B testing imaginable.

Gross margin

Gross margin is a company's total sales revenue minus the cost of products/ service it has sold, divided by the total sales revenue, expressed as a percentage.

G

The gross margin represents the percentage of total sales revenue that the company retains after incurring direct costs associated with producing the goods and services sold by the company.

Gross margin contribution

In accounting, the £ sterling amount that a purchase adds to the gross margin after subtracting all variable costs. In conversion optimisation gross margin is often used instead of profit since the design of the website rarely has any impact on the difference between margin and profit.

Grouping

We group stimuli to form a unified picture or impression of a product/service.

Growth hacking

Using content marketing, A/B testing, and analytics to enable quick, efficient business growth.

Growth optimisation

Growth optimisation goes beyond basic conversion rate optimisation (CRO). CRO is only part of it. Instead growth optimisation uses a multidisciplinary approach (data scientists, psychologists, writers, analysts, designers, developers, CX experts, and market researchers) to grow revenue by helping companies:

- Gain an in-depth and continually updated understanding of their website visitors and customers
- Understand where they fit in the market
- Gain a clearer and more business critical view of how data can help improve a business and make it agile
- Establish an intelligence-based approach to their online business.

This process enables growth by finding the opportunities that will provide major impact in increasing revenue within a business.

Guerrilla testing

Form of testing/research done quickly or without a completely rigorous process.

Guest checkout option

This is a checkout option designed to allow people to buy without having to create an account.

Gutenberg diagram

Developed by typographer Edmund C. Arnold. Product webpages in particular follow the basis of the model. It helps to explain reading gravity and is based on a concept that people "zone" what they're looking at into four areas as they scan from the left to right and back again (in a z-shaped pattern). Although there is little evidence to support that it improves user experience, the diagram has established itself as a universal design principle.

The Gutenberg Diagram suggests how we scan across a page through the axis of orientation and under the influence of "reading gravity".

SEE FIGURE 20

The diagram can be explained as follows:

1. The primary optical focus area — the first place a visitor will look in a left-to-right webpage scanning scenario. Logos are placed here to reassure them that they've arrived at the right place and anything else that should stimulate the interest and keep them on their scent trail is positioned here too.
2. The strong fallow area — is used for the login button, registration form CTA, help link, shipping, basket, etc.
3. The weak fallow area — nothing important is placed here.
4. The terminal area — where CTAs, purchasing buttons, links and so forth, are located.

This is not a rule. Test webpages to find out what works for the website's users.

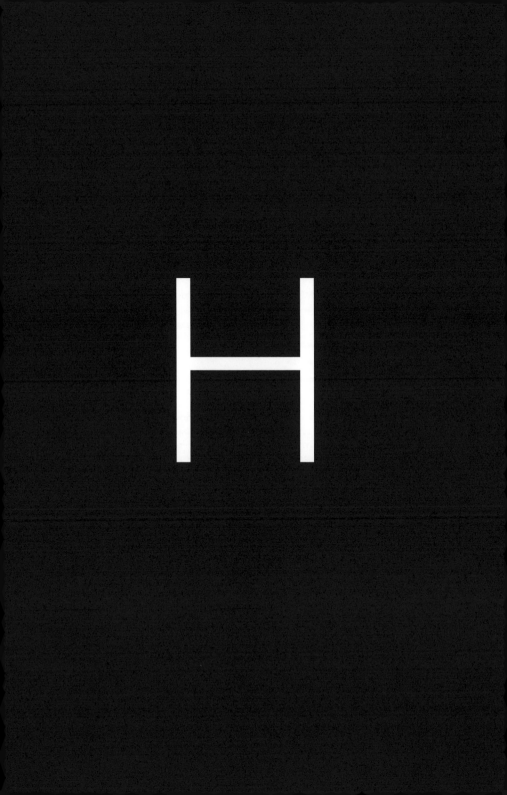

H

Habituation
When a stimulus becomes too familiar and loses its ability to get attention.

Hack
A quick and dirty approach to problem-solving. A hacker is a free-thinker and is unafraid to break rules in search of the right answer.

Halo effect
This is a cognitive bias in which a person's overall impression of another person or object influences how they feel and think about them.

Hamburger
A menu icon commonly represented by three stacked lines.

Happy talk
Promotional writing that adds nothing to the website visitor's experience. It doesn't provide useful, informative content.

Hashtag
Used on social media sites, a hashtag is a word or phrase preceded by a hash sign (#) to identify posts on a specific topic.

HCI
Human computer interaction involves the study, planning, and design of the interaction between people and computers.

Headings
A heading is made up of a word, phrase or sentence that appears at the start of a section of written text (e.g., <h1>Use Data and Psychology to Optimise Your Site</h1>). Its purpose is to explain what that section of text is about. In HTML, six levels of headings can be defined; H1 through to H6 where H1 equates to first level heading

of the document. H2 to H6 can be used to further define the structure of the document. This is an example:

<h1>Earth</h1>

<h2>Europe</h2>

<h3>UK</h3>

<h4>England</h4>

<h5>Manchester</h5>

<h6>Portland Street</h6>

Correct definition of headings and page elements such as paragraphs and lists, allow developers to create semantic mark-up that separates the visual presentation of information from the actual content. Semantic webpages are easier to use, have greater accessibility, are easier to maintain and are search engine friendly.

Headlines
Headlines indicate the nature of the whole text that follows them. These need to be meaningful and engaging — importantly they need to be unambiguous and accurate. Headlines that work well summarise the text beneath it *(e.g., Use Data and Psychology to Optimise Your Site)*.

Heatmap
Graphical representation of data captured from user interactions as they scan a webpage or use a mouse or stylus to click on various things. *See also Eye tracking and Mouse tracking.*

SEE FIGURE 13

Heatseeker
A person who can be relied on to buy the most up to date version of an existing product as soon as it's available. This has implications for companies selling high-demand products, as they need to have

resilient, fast website hosting to cope with vast increases in traffic.

Hero shot
The main image or a video on a webpage that persuasively shows a product being used as intended.

Heuristic analysis
Heuristic analysis asks questions of a website. It is conducted by an experienced optimiser who will follow the path a user would take on a website. Along this path they ask questions of each page of a website to see if it fulfils its objectives. For example, does the product listing page help the user find the product that is right for them.

Heuristic Systematic Model (HSM)
HSM attempts to explain how people receive and process persuasive messages. It suggests that individuals can process messages either heuristically or systematically. It is thought that people minimise their use of cognitive resources, which affects their message intake and processing ability. HSM is quite similar to the elaboration likelihood model (ELM) with which it shares comparable concepts.

SEE FIGURE 21

Hick's law (Hick-Hyman law)
The time it takes to make a decision increases proportionally to the number and complexity of choices. Hick's law is the appropriate model in choosing an alternative from a menu or navigation bar for decision times, *rather than Miller's "magic number" of seven, plus or minus two (see definition).*

Hidden form
A form that has been completed by someone other than the customer, often done on their behalf because they aren't the person actually paying for the product/service. Can also refer to an unofficial form completed and sent in, which is subsequently input into the official version by customer services.

Hidden target
A target that is difficult to find. These show up in eye tracking experiments where a participant does not fixate on the target. Instead they perform long, complex gaze paths and either fixate on an incorrect target or they give up.

Hierarchy
The order in which the eye perceives what it sees on a webpage. Webpages have to be tested to offer the correct hierarchy in order to help customers with selecting and buying products.

Hierarchy of effects
The steps we take to make a decision: Thinking is followed by feeling, and then behaviour.

High-effort hierarchy of effects
A purchase made following significant decision-making effort.

High-fidelity prototype
Interactive prototype that simulates the real system or website's functionality and design. *See also low-fidelity prototype.*

HiPPO
Highest paid person's opinion.

Hippocampus
The part of the brain that is responsible for memory forming, organising, and moving short-term memories to long-term storage.

History effect
History effects occur when external factors interfere with tests and challenge their validity. Think marketing campaigns, holiday seasons — Christmas, Easter, etc., the various seasons themselves, good/bad PR involving the company or industry, product recalls and so on.

H

Hit
This is an interaction that results in data being sent to Google Analytics. Common types include webpage tracking hits, event hits, ecommerce hits, etc.

Home page
The initial main webpage of a website.

Honey pot technique
This is an alternative to annoying captchas on forms. It uses CSS to hide a form field from the user that is supposed to be left blank. Bot's ignore the CSS! Each time a form is submitted, the field can be checked to see if it's blank; if it's not, mark it as spam.

Hook
In copywriting, a hook is used to grab website visitor's attention. Generally, the website or product's USP is highlighted to gain their interest.

Hooked model
Nir Eyal's hooked model describes how to convert external triggers that engage a person with a product into internal triggers that bring them back to it repeatedly.

SEE FIGURE 22

Hover help
Usually a smaller box with information that appears or pops up if a user puts their mouse over a designated graphical or text element. See also Tool tip.

HTML (hyper text markup language)
A markup language used for displaying webpages and applications in web browsers. It uses markup tags to describe webpages, and each tag describes different content.

Human factors (ergonomics)
The scientific discipline of studying interactions between humans and external systems, including human-computer interaction. When applied to design, the study of human factors seeks to optimise both human well-being and system performance.

Hyperbolic discounting
Refers to how people tend to prefer early rewards. So hyperbolic discounting plays to the likelihood of people choosing smaller, earlier rewards rather than waiting for a bigger reward that won't arrive until much later.

Hypothesis
Sometimes referred to as a test hypothesis. An informed theory or assumption that can be proved or disproved by measurable observations. For example,

- Because we saw (qualitative and quantitative data)
- We expect that (change) for (population) will cause (impact[s])
- We expect to see (data metric(s) change) over a period of (x business cycles)", *Craig Sullivan.*

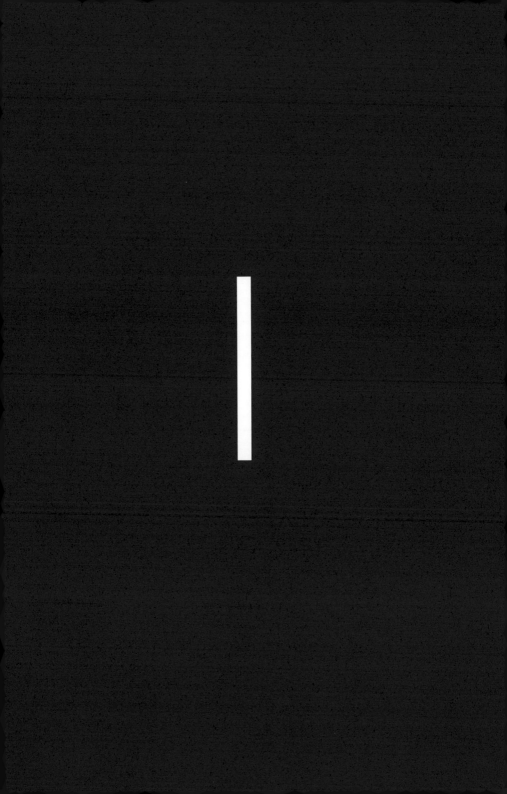

Icon

Symbol or image representing something more complex like a "hamburger" navigation button. Also refers to a role-model or a product that is thought standard setting/ground breaking.

Iconic memory

A brief memory of what we see.

Ideal identity schema

A set of ideas about how one would ideally like to be.

Ideal state

The way we'd like things to be.

IKEA (labour-love) effect

People place greater value on something they have had to invest time and effort in.

Illusory correlation

Perceiving a relationship between variables when there isn't one.

Imagery

What we create in our minds so that we can make a judgment.

Imagery processing

Processing information in sensory form.

Immediate feedback

People are actively engaged in their tasks when their actions get instant responses from the website. It encourages them to continue on their scent trail. For example, progress bars on forms let people know where they are in the form filling process, dynamic filters for onsite navigation, allowing customers to add their reviews in real-time, etc.

Implicit memory

Unconscious memory that draws on past experiences to remember things without actually thinking about them (those things that are done automatically).

Implicit motive

The unconscious needs that drive an individual to complete an action.

Impulse purchase

An unplanned purchase triggered by seeing something that creates an emotional response and desire to buy.

Inattentional blindness (perceptual blindness)

When a person does not recognise something unexpected that is in plain sight.

Inbound marketing

Marketing efforts that use content to draw people to a website, such as blogs and social networks, also emails to existing subscribers/customers who have confirmed that they are happy to receive communications.

Incentive

Incentives can be added to a website to encourage visitors to take action and buy, e.g., next day delivery if they buy now, discounts, etc. See also Discounts.

Incidental learning

Unplanned learning that occurs when carrying out an action or observing others.

Independent variable

A test variable (e.g. a treatment) that can be controlled and isn't dependent on other variables.

Indirect response copywriting

Copywriting that introduces a potential customer to a product/service. It informs them about the product/service and its benefits with the aim that they'll remember and eventually buy it.

Industrial design

Applying art and science to a product to improve its aesthetics, ergonomics, functionality, and usability.

Inept set

Brands (or products/services, etc.) that people think poorly of when making a purchasing decision.

Inference

Using evidence to reach a conclusion.

Inferential statistics

Drawing conclusions about a population from a representative sample.

Information architecture (IA)

Information architecture refers to the organising, structuring, and labelling of website content to help users find information and complete tasks. Those in charge of designing, creating and developing a website should understand how the various pieces of content work together and how they relate to one another within the website.

Information foraging

What people do when they visit a website. They use their information scent to estimate how successful they will be. If successful, the visit may end in a sale/subscription. *See also Scent trail.*

Information overload

Too much information getting in the way of, or hampering, decision making.

Informational social influence

Social proof can influence the buying decision by providing reassuring information to the consumer.

Inline validation

This can reduce friction in forms by giving real-time feedback to the person filling out the form. It stops them from giving the wrong information by confirming that the answer is appropriate to the question asked, also suggesting valid answers, where appropriate, etc.

Inline validation provides users with real-time responses such as confirming they have given an appropriate answer, proposing valid answers, and providing regular updates to help them keep within necessary limits. Such feedback can be provided either before, during and/or after the user has answered a question.

For example, once the user has entered information into a form field, validate their answer with a tick mark, or if it's wrong tell them how to correct it.

Innovation

A product/service that is recognised as being new/revolutionary, which can lead to changing buying habits.

In-page analytics

These highlight behaviour metrics for specific webpages.

Input variables (independent variables)

Landing page tests use input variables that can be controlled and manipulated, and output variables (dependent variables) that are observed and measured.

Instant gratification

Experiencing an immediately positive feeling as a result of an action.

Instore impact

How the online experience can impact instore behaviour of customers (driving visits, sales, price checking, etc.).

Instrumental values

Also known as extrinsic values and contributory values. Relates to the value of physical and abstract objects, not as ends-in-themselves, but as means of achieving something else. Also, specific methods of behaviour. Character traits and personal characteristics, such as being imaginative, independent, cheerful, focused, etc.

Instrumentation effect

When incorrect tracking is inserted on a website it will suffer from an instrumentation effect. It's a common error that harms results. It can be avoided by ensuring time is taken when setting up the test and by scrutinising the implementation with great care. It is important to ensure that every goal and metric that is to be tracked is closely monitored and confirmed that they are being recorded by the analytics package.

Integration of evidence

Enhancing our evidence by adding new information to our stored knowledge.

Intellectual property (IP)

A term for any valuable but intangible asset that doesn't exist as a physical object. For example, it covers designs, concepts, software, inventions, trade secrets, formulas, and brand names. Note that protecting IP must go beyond protecting a website's design and content. It should also cover testimonials and reviews written by customers as companies may like to use their words and images (if appropriate) in their advertising and marketing. So, ensure that customers' content that is posted or written on a website can be used and is covered by the website's terms and conditions.

Intelligence events alerts

Google Analytics generates automatic web alerts whenever it detects a significant change in a website's usage or traffic metrics. There are also automatic AdWords alerts when Google Analytics detects a significant change in traffic from AdWords. Custom alerts can be set up for when traffic reaches a specific threshold.

Interaction design (IxD)

Interaction design or IxD aims at creating meaningful relationships between people and products and services that they use.

Interaction model

A design model that binds an application together in a way that supports the conceptual models of its target users. It's how all of the objects and actions that are part of an application interrelate in ways that mirror and support real-life user interactions. Therefore, the user should be able to complete similar tasks in the same way all over a website or in an app.

Interference

When information about competing products/services is closely aligned people get confused about which features/benefits go with which.

Interloper effect

A cognitive bias where people tend to value third-party, expert reviews on websites as being objective and trustworthy. This is in addition to testimonials from customers, i.e., if an external expert says a product/service is good, it must be good!

Internal search

When people actively recall stored information from their memory.

Also refers to onsite searching (and associated Google Analytics or other platform reports). Some people will use the internal/onsite search engine, rather than use the website navigation. Internal search is a good option if a website has more than 30 products.

Internationalisation

A system whose primary design has been developed to work in multiple languages and in the cultural contexts of different locales.

Internesia

Inability to find/recall a particular website that was of previous interest or contained a useful piece of information.

Interruption

A technique used to grab the website visitors' attention by intentionally interrupting their user experience. It needs careful application to avoid having the opposite, negative effect of driving them away.

Interviews

One-on-one interactions between end-users and researchers to gather data.

Intrinsic motivation

This is when a person does something because they choose to do it. It is possible to maximise visitors' intrinsic motivation by ensuring that the website is attractive and absorbing. See also Extrinsic motivation.

Intrinsically photosensitive retinal ganglion cells

These photosensitive cells in the eye respond to light in the absence of all rod and cone photoreceptor input. They help synchronise our physiology and behaviour according to daylight and darkness. They also provide signals to the brain for non-imaging functions such as pupil light reflex.

Intuitive

When something is easy to do — without any coaching or directing — it is said to be intuitive. For example, if a website claims to offer an intuitive experience, as soon as a visitor sees the interface they should know exactly what to do. However, what may be intuitive to one person (based on his/her experience) may be counter-intuitive to another person so it is important to test what is assumed to be intuitive to ensure it really is.

Invasive questions

It is important that websites avoid asking for more personal data on web forms than is absolutely needed to fulfil the needs of website visitors/customers. They will question why it is being asked for and if they aren't happy to give it they may abandon the website and what's in their shopping baskets.

Inventory

Describes a retailer's current stock and (sometimes) its value. Inventory levels are checked regularly, to manage shrinkage and minimum order levels, and to prevent promoting out-of-stock products.

Inverted pyramid

A copywriting style that is applied to websites that places the most important information at the top of the page where it is most likely to be seen. This is especially important as people on the web don't read, they scan and 80 per cent of people don't scroll down past the fold. See Fold.

Italics

Use sparingly for emphasis within a sentence, for example. Other uses are for book/magazine/event titles. But, whole sentences or blocks of italic text can be difficult to scan/read. See also Legibility, Readability, and Typography.

Iterate

The act of repeating a process with the aim of approaching a desired goal, target or result. Each repetition of the process is also called an iteration.

Iterative design

This is the process of prototyping, testing, analysing, and refining a website, webpage, checkout, etc., continually until an optimal design is achieved. Each version — iteration — of the design is tested and improvements made based on the results.

Iterative testing

Repeat testing of a treatment enabling adjustments/improvements to the test hypothesis and webpage until a desired outcome is achieved.

FIGURE 1
Above the fold, Below the fold and Fold

The fold divides what can be seen when first looking at a web page (above the fold) with what can't be seen because it requires the user to scroll down (below the fold).

Above the fold
Important content, e.g.,
value proposition, logo,
navigation and search

The fold

Below the fold
Auxiliary content

FIGURE 2
A/B testing (split testing)

A/B testing compares two versions of a webpage or app — the original or control "A" and its variant "B" — against each other to determine which one performs better.

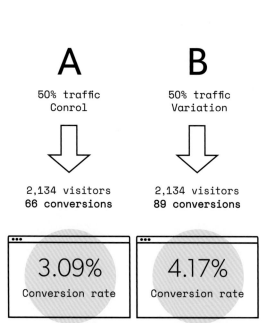

A   # B

50% traffic   50% traffic
Conrol   Variation

2,134 visitors   2,134 visitors
66 conversions   89 conversions

3.09%   4.17%
Conversion rate   Conversion rate

FIGURE 3
Analogous colours

Analogous colours are those positioned next to a given colour on a colour wheel e.g., pink, purple, and violet. These tend to harmonise with each other and are pleasing to the eye.

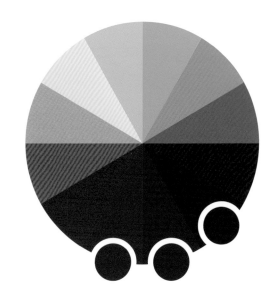

FIGURE 4
Awareness alerts

Awareness alerts use things such as disruptive visual cues to draw attention to important information, and use relevant content and/or popups that challenge subconscious decisions, e.g.: *"Are you sure you want to cancel your subscription?"*

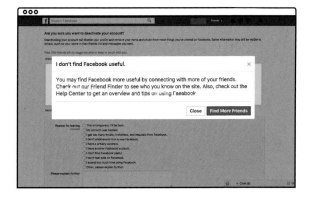

FIGURE 5
Basket recovery

Actively attempting to recover the sale once the user has abandoned the purchase process.

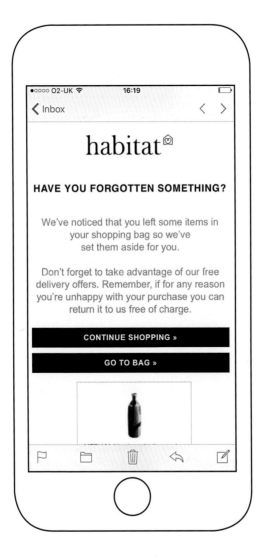

FIGURE 6
Choice paradox

Presenting too many options can result in fewer choices taken by website visitors, in fact they may leave without making a choice. Choice requires them to use the conscious System 2 part of their brains but this can only typically choose between about five options.

Search results

100 results for 'vienna cruise'

Vienna to Budapest | Olympia Danube River Cruise | Newmarket ...

Cruise the Danube visiting Vienna, Budapest and the Slovakian capital Bratislava. Book your Olympia Danube River Cruise with confidence from Newmarket ...

Vienna, Budapest & Bratislava | Sound of Music Danube River ...

Visit Vienna, Budapest and Bratislava on this river cruise along the Danube. Book your Sound of Music Danube River Cruise with confidence from Newmarket ...

Danube Cruise to Vienna & Budapest with Flights - 2016 - 8 days ...

Join Olympia as she journeys along one of the world's most iconic rivers, through historic Vienna, stunning Budapest and enchanting Bratislava.

Vienna, Budapest & Bratislava | Sound of Music River Cruise ...

Visit Antwerp, Brussels and Ghent, and see the vibrant spring gardens at Keukenhof. Book your Sound of Music River Cruise with confidence from Newmarket ...

Olympia Rhine River Cruises 2017 | Newmarket Holidays

Olympia Rhine River Cruises 2017 - Meet at Port. Danube Cruise to Vienna & Budapest 2017. 10 days from. £989. per person. More info. Olympia Rhine River ...

Danube, Main & Rhine | Sound of Music River Cruise | Newmarket ...

Sail from Vienna and cruise three iconic rivers - the Danube, Main and Rhine. Book your Sound of Music River Cruise with confidence from Newmarket ...

River Cruises

Danube Cruise to Vienna and Budapest, Olympia, Sept 2017, Fly from regional UK airports, 8 days, £1219, Danube Cruise to Vienna and Budapest. Coach from ...

Cologne to Strasbourg | Olympia Rhine River Cruise | Newmarket ...

... visit Freiburg. Book your Olympia Rhine River Cruise with confidence from Newmarket Holidays. ... Danube Cruise to Vienna & Budapest 2017. 10 days from.

Prague, Budapest and Vienna 2016-2017 | Holiday Europe ...

Visit Prague, enjoy a river cruise in Budapest and take a guided tour of Imperial Vienna. Book your European holiday with confidence from Newmarket Holidays.

The Spanish Riding School of Vienna in London - 2016 - 2-day ...

FIGURE 7
Decoy effect

Also known as the "Ugly twin effect", after Dan Ariely. This can be useful for upselling (making the higher priced item look better value than the cheapest) and for decoy selling where similar products with similar prices but different brands are available. It can be used to persuade visitors to see a specific product (or a website) as a more attractive option than the one it's being compared against.

BELOW:
1. The "Ugly twin"
experiment by
Dan Ariely.
2. Decoy pricing.

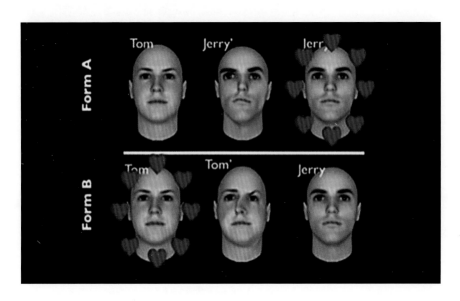

FIGURE 8
Drop down label/menu

A drop down menu is a graphical control or a navigational element that allows website visitors to select one value from a list and enables information capture e.g., number of guests. If there are too many options, however, a drop down list can become a usability issue. Test before implementing.

FIGURE 9
Eisenberg Hierarchy of Conversion

This conversion optimisation theory explains that when people visit a website, they enter at the bottom of a pyramid of needs. When the base needs at the bottom of the pyramid are met, potential customers can move up to address the next need.

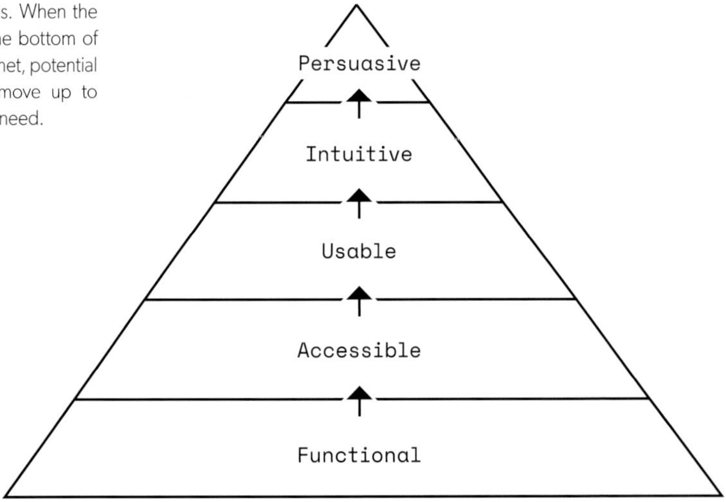

Persuasive

Intuitive

Usable

Accessible

Functional

FIGURE 10
Elaboration Likelihood Model

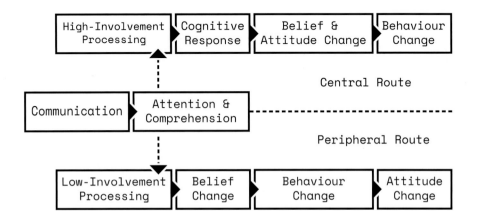

This psychological model aims to explain different ways of processing stimuli, why they are used, and their outcomes on attitude change.

It proposes two major routes to persuasion: the central route (now known as System 2) and the peripheral route (now known as System 1).

Source: Petty, R.E. and Cacioppo, J.T. (1986). The Elaboration Likelihood Model of persuasion. New York Academic Press.

FIGURE 11
Extended Parrallel Process Model

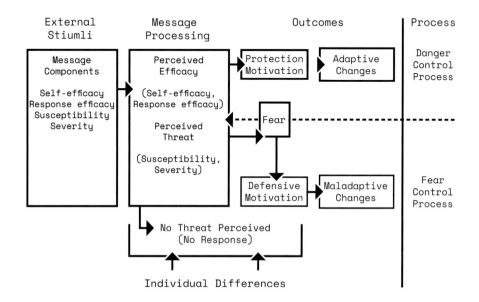

This model attempts to predict how individuals will react when confronted by fear-inducing stimuli. It is commonly used in encouraging people to adopt a healthy behaviour, e.g., quit smoking, eat more fruit and vegetables, get screened for a disease, etc. For fear-based campaigns to be effective, they must induce a moderately-high level of fear and a higher level of self-efficacy and response-efficacy. If the level of fear is too high or not high enough, the message is ineffective.

Source: Witte, K. (1994). Fear control and danger control: A test of the extended parallel process model. Communication Monographs, 61(2), 113-134.

FIGURE 12
Eye

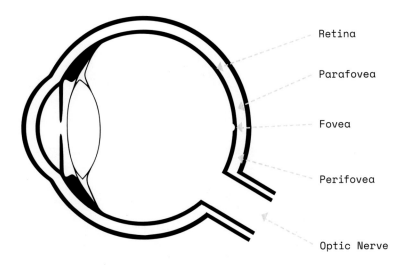

Retina

Parafovea

Fovea

Perifovea

Optic Nerve

A specialised organ that reacts to light
and enables vision. The lens focuses on an
object and the retina captures the image,
resulting in chemical and electrical events
that send nerve impulses to the brain's
visual cortex through the optic nerve.

FIGURE 13
Eye tracking

Heat maps show the accumulated time that test participants spent looking at the different areas of the webpage.

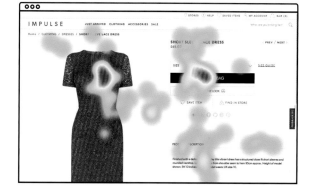

Gaze plots show a test participant's fixations as dots, and saccades as lines. The size of the dots represents the length of fixation — so the bigger the dot, the longer the fixation. The number of dots and their sizes seen in a gaze plot is dependent on the parameters of the test.

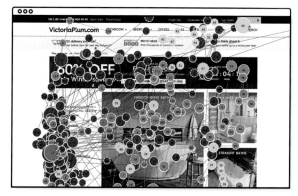

Time to first fixation is the amount of time that it takes a person to look at a specific AOI on a webpage or app. This can be measured with eye tracking. Understanding the time to first fixation data can inform a better customer experience.

FIGURE 14
Facial Distraction

The brain is programmed from an early age to scan faces. In doing so, people can miss other persuasive information on website product pages because they are distracted by focusing on the face of a model, for example.

BELOW: The images of the model's face are competing with the product and CTA.

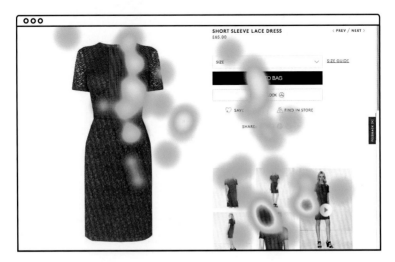

FIGURE 15
Figure and ground

How people interpret stimuli in the context of a background
(Gestalt psychology). This is vital for recognising objects
using eyesight, such as recognising words on a page. The
figure could be interpreted as two faces looking towards
each other with a white background or a chalice in front of
a black background.

FIGURE 16
Fogg Behaviour Model

Behaviour = Motivation + Ability + Trigger, or B = MAT.
All of those elements must happen at the "same moment"
to elicit the behaviour. *See also Yerkes-Dodson Law, which
describes correlation between arousal and performance.*

Source: behaviourmodel.org

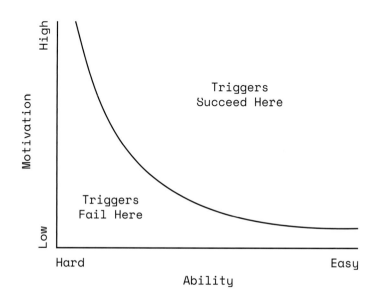

FIGURE 17
Foveal vision

This is just 1° of a person's entire 180° field of vision beyond direct line of sight, which is processed by the fovea in each eye. To get an idea of the coverage, hold an arm out straight and look at the thumbnail — when people look at a website that is the total area of what they will see in fine detail. This has implications for the positioning of webpage elements.

FIGURE 18
F-pattern

The F-pattern is how people are thought to view webpages. It was the discovery of Jakob Nielsen, Nielsen Norman Group.

FIGURE 19
Funnel

A funnel helps with visualising and comprehending the customer journey through a website before finally converting to a sale. Funnel describes the decrease in numbers that occurs at each step of the process, thereby indicating areas for optimising.

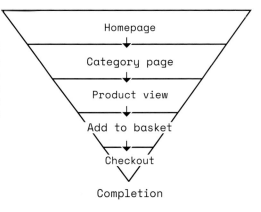

FIGURE 20
Gutenberg Diagram

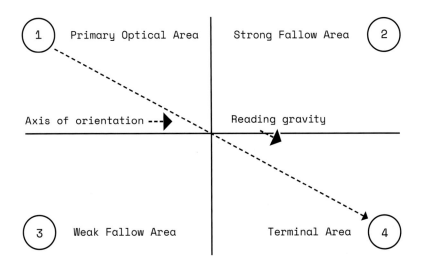

The Gutenberg Diagram suggests how we scan across a page through the axis of orientation and under the influence of "reading gravity":

1. **The Primary Optical Area** — the first place a visitor will look in a left-to-right webpage scanning scenario. Logos are placed here to reassure them that they've arrived at the right place and anything else that should stimulate the interest and keep them on their scent trail is positioned here too.
2. **The Strong Fallow Area** — is used for the login button, registration form CTA, help link, shipping, basket, etc.
3. **The Weak Fallow Area** — nothing important is placed here.
4. **The Terminal Area** — where CTAs, purchasing buttons, links and so forth, are located.

FIGURE 21
Heuristic Systematic Model

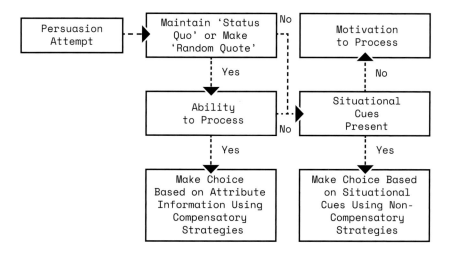

The Heuristic Systematic Model (HSM) attempts to explain how people receive and process persuasive messages. It suggests that individuals can process messages either heuristically or systematically. It is thought that people minimise their use of cognitive resources, which affects their message intake and processing ability. HSM is quite similar to the elaboration likelihood model (ELM) with which it shares comparable concepts.

Source: Chaiken, S. (1980). Heuristic Vs Systematic Information Processing and the Use of Source Versus Message Cues in Persuasion. The Journal of Personality and Social Psychology, 39(5), 752-766.

FIGURE 22
Hooked Model

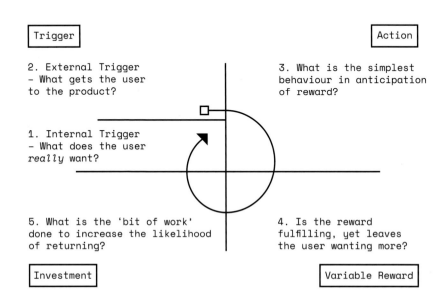

Trigger

2. External Trigger
- What gets the user
to the product?

1. Internal Trigger
- What does the user
really want?

Action

3. What is the simplest
behaviour in anticipation
of reward?

5. What is the 'bit of work'
done to increase the likelihood
of returning?

4. Is the reward
fulfilling, yet leaves
the user wanting more?

Investment

Variable Reward

Nir Eyal's Hooked Model describes how
to convert external triggers that engage a
person with a product into internal triggers
that bring them back to it repeatedly.

Source: nirandfar.com/hooked

FIGURE 23
Reflective-Impulsive Model

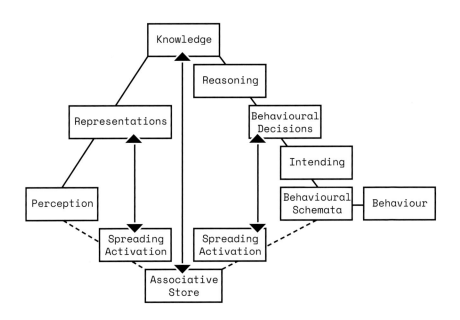

The Reflective-Impulsive Model is the first dual process model that incorporates both System 1 and System 2. It explains social behaviour as a joint function of reflective and impulsive processes. Here two interacting systems, that operate differently from each other, control social behaviour.

The reflective system (System 2) uses facts and values to make behavioural decisions.

The impulsive system (System 1) causes behaviour by associative links (connections between memories) and motivational orientation that define a particular action.

Source: Strack, F., and Deutsch, R. (2004). Reflective and impulsive determinants of social behavior. Personality and Social Psychology Review, 8 (3), 220-247.

FIGURE 24
Stroop effect

BLUE YELLOW BLACK
RED BLUE ORANGE
GREEN PURPLE RED
BLACK RED ORANGE
GREEN BLUE BLACK
RED PURPLE YELLOW

A demonstration to highlight interference in the reaction times of a task. It is often used to highlight the conflict between our dual processing brain (Systems 1 and 2). For example, name the colour of the words, but do not read the words.

Source: Stroop, J.R. (1935). Studies of interference in serial verbal reactions. Journal of Experimental Psychology.

FIGURE 25
System 1 and System 2

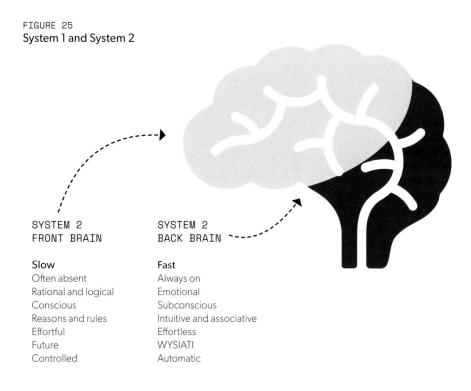

SYSTEM 2 FRONT BRAIN	SYSTEM 2 BACK BRAIN
Slow	**Fast**
Often absent	Always on
Rational and logical	Emotional
Conscious	Subconscious
Reasons and rules	Intuitive and associative
Effortful	Effortless
Future	WYSIATI
Controlled	Automatic

FIGURE 26

Type I error

The incorrect rejection of a true null hypothesis (false positive). Essentially detecting an effect that is not present.

Type II error

The incorrect rejection of a true alternative hypothesis retaining a false null hypothesis (false negative). Failing to detect an effect that is present.

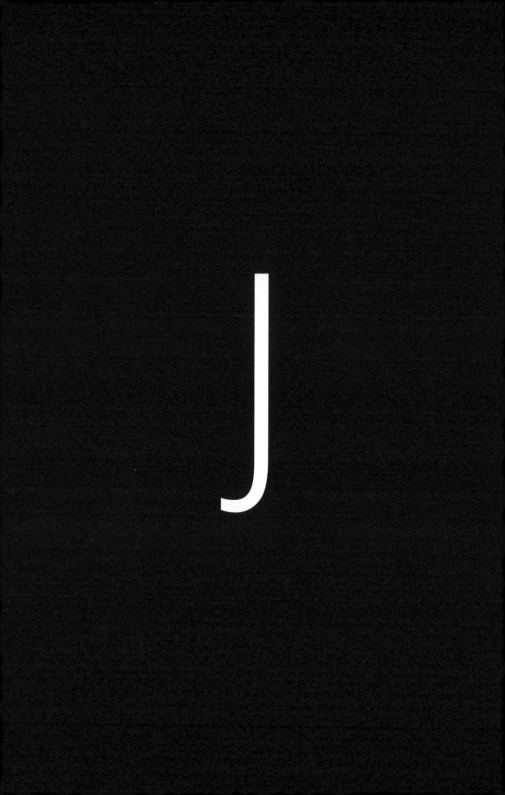

James-Lange theory of emotion

A peripheral-feedback theory of emotion stating that an eliciting stimulus triggers a behavioural response that sends different sensory and motor feedback to the brain and creates the feeling of a specific emotion. Seeing a particular product on a webpage causes a gut feeling about it, for example. The webpage, therefore, needs to cater for the emotion to reassure the visitor about the product.

Jargon

Words/phrases used by organisations that are difficult for external people to understand. Using jargon on a website can be limiting unless it is being used specifically for a certain target audience that understands it.

Jarrett-Zetie rules of popups

- Expectation: The user expects new content and expects that content to be a diversion from the current task rather than intrinsic to it
- Context: There is some advantage to the user in seeing the new content on screen at the same time as the existing content
- Size: The popup size is between one quarter and one third of the existing window size. If the size is less than one quarter, then the content should be moved on to the main page. If the size is more than one third, then you break the rule of context
- Knowledge: The user isn't thrown by popups and knows how to close them
- Obvious single use: There is only one popup at a time, and you have some way of being sure that the popup comes to the front.

In C Jarrett and G Gaffney, "Forms that work", Morgan Kaufmann, Elsevier (2009).

JavaScript

A popular programming language that's built into all the major web browsers and is used to make webpages interactive.

JDI (Just Do It)

Refers to fixing obvious problems discovered during conversion research or bug testing that do not require further investigating or testing.

Joint Advisory Design (JAD) sessions

Meetings in which developers and users collaborate to discuss aspects of an interface under development.

Journey

The end-to-end series of steps a visitor/customer takes to complete a specific task — for example, the steps they take to purchase a product from a website.

Joystick

Not just for gamers, specialist joysticks are a type of assistive technology that acts as a pointing device. They can be large or small depending on the purpose they are being applied to and are useful for people who have a relatively severe physical disability such as cerebral palsy.

JPEG/JPG

An image file type that uses "lossy" compression to reduce the size of the file without much visible loss in quality. It is used generally for photographs.

jQuery

A "lightweight" JavaScript library, the purpose of which is to make it easier to use JavaScript on your website.

Judgements

When the likelihood of an event is estimated/evaluated. Also, judging the desirability of a product/service.

J

K

Kahneman (Daniel)

Nobel Memorial Prize in Economic Sciences winner, Daniel Kahneman is regarded as the thought leader in System 1 and System 2 brain theory. Author of *"Thinking, Fast and Slow"*, a book that summarises the research he performed over several decades. *See System 1 and System 2, and Dual process theory.*

Kerning

The adjustment of space between two characters in type. Kerning usually aims to achieve a more proportional and pleasing balance of space between each character and is important for headlines and display type. It also helps with visual fluency.

Keyword

A word or phrase typed into the search box on either a search engine or a website. It is important that the webpage the visitor is taken to, once they have clicked on the related link, supports the keyword they have typed in. This lets the visitor know they are on the right scent. *See also Scent trail.*

Keyword research

Finding the actual search terms that people enter into search engines.

Keyword stuffing

According to Google, "Keyword stuffing refers to the practice of loading a webpage with keywords or numbers in an attempt to manipulate a website's ranking in Google search results. Often these keywords appear in a list or group, or out of context (not as natural prose). Filling pages with keywords or numbers results in a negative user experience, and can harm your website's ranking. Focus on creating useful, information-rich content that uses keywords appropriately and in context." *See also Black hat techniques.*

Kicker

An optional short summary phrase used above a headline. The idea being to create more impact.

KLM-GOMS

Part of the GOMS family of predictive models, the Keystroke-Level Model GOMS (KLM-GOMS [goals, operators, methods, selection rules]) is a quantitative modelling tool for predicting how long it will take expert users to complete a specific task with no errors.

Knowledge (curse of)

This refers to knowing too much about a product, service or any other topic to be able to communicate effectively with customers. So, it makes it necessary for all websites to get on the same level as their customers.

Knowledge content

The information we have in our memory.

Knowledge structure

The way in which we organise our stored information.

KPI

A key performance indicator (KPI) is a business metric used to evaluate factors that are crucial to the success of an organisation.

K

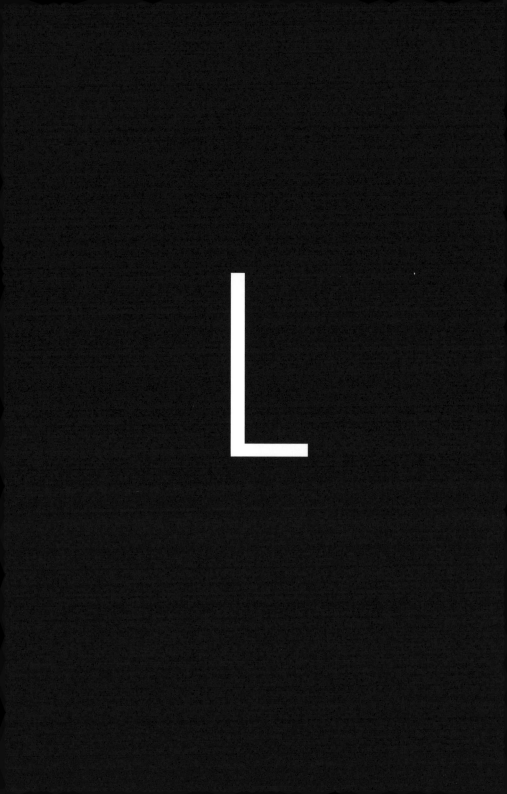

Lab(oratory)

Facility that provides controlled conditions in which scientific or technological research, experiments, and measurements may be performed.

Labels

Labels refer to questions on checkout, subscription and survey forms that identify the fields that the visitor/customer has to fill out using specific details. When labelling forms, position them so that they associate closely with the appropriate fields. Tests show that labels positioned above the form fields work the best. However, there are always exceptions, so always test label positioning.

Labour-love effect

A cognitive bias that encourages people to put higher value on a product that they have invested time and effort in. *See also IKEA effect.*

Landing page

The location in a website where a given user arrives at after clicking on an external link. Also known as a target page or destination page. Landing pages are often in response to a link in an online advert or email, or a specific URL displayed by an offline advert/flyer/brochure.

Latency

The time measured in milliseconds between a stimulus and its response.

Latent clickthrough

When web users see an online banner advert but don't visit the advertised website immediately. It is only a latent clickthrough if the web user does not click directly on the banner.

Latent conversion

A type of conversion that takes place after a visitor's initial visit. For example, someone may look for a price, leave the website to think about it, come back to the website two days later, and then make a purchase.

Last click attribution

The most commonly used attribution model that awards the credit for a sale/conversion to the source of the most recent click to the website.

Lateral geniculate nucleus (LGN)

Is a relay centre in the thalamus for the visual pathway.

It receives major sensory input from the retina, processes it, making it ready for the brain to pass the information to the primary visual cortex.

Launch page

A webpage that announces the upcoming arrival of a new website, product, etc. It is often referred to as a coming soon page.

Law of distraction

This refers to how a distracted person is more likely to fail at completing a task successfully. This is because the rational part of the brain (System 2) doesn't like distractions. On a webpage it is important, therefore, to remove distractions (unnecessary navigation, social sharing buttons, banners, offers, etc.) from a defined task such as responding to a call to action.

Law of small numbers

The questionable assumption that the characteristics of a sample population can be estimated from a small number of observations or data points.

Layering

A method of organising and dividing information for website visitors. The idea is to show information about a product or service in additional layers, such as popups, roll overs or secondary windows that open when the visitor points at a more information CTA, for example. It prevents visitors from being overwhelmed with information.

L

Lead
A potential customer who has supplied contact information.

Lead generation
Initiation of consumer interest or inquiry into products or services of a business. It typically uses a computer program, a database, the Internet, or a specialised service to obtain or receive information for the purpose of increasing sales revenues. For example, websites may offer something in return for an email address.

Leading
Pronounced "led-ing". This refers to the space between lines of type. Overly tight leading can cause tension and overlap, making the content difficult to read, and too-loose leading can equally make the type appear disjointed, so it is best to try to find a balance between the two.

L

Leakages
Refers to losing customers and, therefore, money from a website. Conversion research identifies the leakages within a website.

Lean start up methodology
A similar process to that used for optimising websites but in this instance it is used to accelerate business growth. *See also Conversion optimisation process.*

Lean UX (user experience)
Inspired by lean and agile development theories, lean UX speeds up the UX process by putting less emphasis on deliverables and greater focus on the actual experience being designed.

Learnability
How easy or difficult it is to learn to use a system or interface effectively.

Legibility
The measure of how easy it is to distinguish one letter from the next. Legibility has a lot to do with the choice of typeface and how it is used, i.e. simpler serif or sans serif typefaces are generally better for smaller body copy. It's also advisable to use a good colour contrast for the font to ensure everyone can read the text.

Length of visit (average time on site)
The measure of the quality of a visit as represented by the length of a session in time. This provides a number in seconds, minutes (and hours) but can be misleading as an average when the range of session length on your website can vary from 1 second to more than 1 hour. Often more usefully expressed as a distribution of the number of visits (and percentage split) for bands of session length in minutes. Useful when paired with measures of page depth as similar but distinctly different methods of understanding visitor behaviour on site. *See also Depth of visit.*

Lexicographic model
People evaluate product characteristics according to their priorities, and they will choose the brand that best satisfies their highest priority characteristics. For example, a consumer may want to buy a smartphone and if all available brands are equal in that person's view, they will choose the one based on what they think is the most important attribute, for example, the camera.

Life time value
This is the prediction of the net profit attributed to the entire future relationship with a customer. Life time value can be referred to as LTV.

Likert scale
A response range for a type of survey question in which a person is asked to agree or disagree with a statement. The scale typically runs from 1 (strongly disagree) to 5 or 7 (strongly agree). With a Likert scale, neither the numerical scores nor the intervals between score values have any intrinsic meaning.

Limbic system or (paleo) mammalian brain

Complex system of nerves and networks in the brain, involving several areas near the edge of the cortex concerned with instinct and mood. It controls the basic emotions (fear, pleasure, anger) and drives (hunger, dominance, care of offspring). The term is falling into disuse in scientific circles, but persists in marketing. *See also Triune brain.*

Limited access

Refers to how people value exclusivity or belonging to a select group. For example, websites can offer "private sales" and "early access" to select groups of customers. It can also work when a website wants to dispose of end-of-range/end-of-life products, where they can offer special exclusive offers to select customers.

Line graph

Used when both axes show variables that have order. Useful for emphasising changes over time, trends, and interactions.

Line length

Refers to how long a line of text is, for example, the length of a sentence. As a rule of thumb, shorter sentences are easier to read.

Linear models

A class of mathematical models that adds and subtracts the effects of all input variables and their combinations to estimate the corresponding value of the output variables.

Link building

Process of gaining back links to a website.

Linking root domain

When a website links to another once or several times it is known as a linking root domain.

Liquid design

A design technique that automatically scales to fit the user's browser.

List fatigue

In email marketing, when the response of a list to an offer or call-to-action declines after repeated mailings.

List of values (LOV)

A measure of nine principal values in consumer behaviour,

1. Sense of belonging
2. Excitement
3. Warm relationship with others
4. Self-respect
5. Being well-respected
6. Self-fulfilment
7. Accomplishment
8. Fun and enjoyment
9. Security.

Live chat/support

Online chat and instant messaging applications provide online assistance to website visitors and can boost service levels and help with conversions.

Live chat transcripts

Transcripts of "live chat" interaction between website visitors/customers and customer service agents. They help with understanding the causes of friction on particular webpages by reviewing the questions they ask.

Load time

The time it takes webpages to load. People aren't likely to wait for a slow loading website. Slow loading websites lose more customers.

Local maximum

When a website has hit the limit of its current design. In its current state, it is as effective as it is ever going to be.

Local navigation

Refers to navigation within a local area of a website or application including sub-site navigation and page-level navigation.

L

Locus of control

The extent to which individuals believe they can control events affecting them. It's how they interpret why things happen.

Logistics

Transporting inventory to retailers or shipping orders to customers. Many ecommerce businesses outsource logistics to specialist companies.

Long tail keywords

Search phrases including several words that describe a search query for specific products/services, for example.

Long term memory

Permanently stored knowledge.

Lorem ipsum

Also known as dummy copy, *"lorem ipsum"* is generic filler text used when the real text is not available. It's used as placeholder text to demonstrate how a design will look once the real body copy has been included.

Loss aversion

Human nature is to avoid losses before pursuing gains. This is a strong impulse deep within the psyche and is probably twice as strong as the need to pursue gains. So, portraying an outcome as a loss can have a bigger impact then phrasing the same outcome as a gain.

Loss-framed language

Language can be loss-framed (e.g., smoking kills) or gain-framed (e.g., quit smoking and live longer). Both of these approaches can be tested to see which has maximum impact with a target audience. *See also Framing.*

Low-effort hierarchy

Purchases based on limited decision-making effort. Replenishing consumable supplies, for example.

L

Low-fidelity prototype

A quick and easy translation of high-level design concepts so that they can be tested. A low-fidelity prototype is produced to indicate which way the product is heading in terms of design and functionality.

Low-traffic websites

Websites that have only small numbers of visitors/transactions. It is not possible to A/B test a low traffic/low transactional website because the sample size will be too small. But it can still be optimised by:

- Measuring everything that can be measured by ensuring the analytics platform is set up correctly, conducting an experienced-based assessment of the website
- Fixing functionality problems
- Ensuring everything is where it ought to be on the website, and
- Performing both qualitative and quantitative research.

Once all the research has been concluded, the website should make live the "big" things that would be tested if sample size allowed — big because there is a need to see significant change in revenue.

Loyalty

A measure of how many times a customer returns to a website. It requires a brand building a long term relationship with each customer so that it becomes their preferred website. Loyalty requires building trust through providing a positive consistent experience. In analytics there are number of metrics used to measure loyalty, including customer lifetime value, repeat customer rate, net promoter score, and redemption rate.

M

Machine learning
Broadly, a method of data analysis that automates analytical model building. It uses algorithms that iteratively learn from data input into a system and continue to learn and adapt as new data is entered. Used by tools and methods in automated optimisation and personalisation platforms.

Macro conversion
The main or primary objective of a website and what visitors are ultimately expected to do. It is dependent on the website, but generally a sale/purchase on an ecommerce website or a lead/member acquisition or an enquiry completion will be classed as a macro conversion.

Magnifier
A form of assistive software technology that allows visually impaired users to "zoom" content being displayed on a computer monitor.

Main effect
A main effect is the effect of one independent variable — for example, using a single column format on forms — on the dependent variable — improving conversions. *See also Variable interaction.*

Managing by exception
A management principle that focuses on problems or deviations from normal behaviour as measured by a set of performance indicators.

Manual tagging/tracking
The process of manually adding parameters to URLs from a specific campaign activity so they can be identified in your analytics platform. Specific parameters will be defined by the analytics platform. For Google Analytics there is a URL builder tool that simplifies the addition of the relevant parameters to the URL or they can be built manually.

Manufacturer part number (MPN)
The identification code of a part can be collected in analytics platforms and reported against as part of performance reviews. *See also SKU.*

Maps
These enable customers to select a geographical region.

Margin
The profit percentage of a sale after the cost of the products and all costs for selling them are accounted for. Margin is essential to understanding the level of profitability for a sale or when examining a product line.

Margin of error
An analytical technique that allows for an acceptable number of errors in an experiment.

Margins
The space around the edge of a page. Increasing or decreasing the size of a page's margins can create a calmer or a tenser design, respectively.

Market
A category of potential buyers for a particular product/service.

Marketese
This hyperbolic copywriting style embellishes the effects or benefits of a product or service in an attempt to make it appear more attractive to the target audience. It frequently uses superlatives and adjectives.

Market maven
Consumers who are up-to-date on products/services and who sells them. They communicate a lot of information to others. They could be high-profile opinion leaders, bloggers and/or vloggers, for example.

M

Market research
A type of research that looks at industry trends and how a product, service, brand, or organisation is performing against a competitive landscape within an industry. Market research generally explores what competitors are doing and how well they are performing.

Marketing
Promoting and selling products or services through market research, sharing information and advertising.

Marketing stimuli
Information about products/services distributed by various means (adverts, direct mail, sales people, etc.) to eventually reach consumers.

Markup validation
This is performed to ensure the HTML of web content is formed correctly and used in a way that it is compliant with HTML specifications. This is important because clean and properly structured code needs to be present to enable assistive technologies to interpret content correctly.

Masthead
The top of a page within a design. Generally, the terms "masthead" and "header" can be used interchangeably, although masthead can indicate an area where the title and specific information of a page is captured. A masthead of a newspaper, for example, includes the name of the paper, the date of publication, and publisher.

Match-up hypothesis
This refers to the practice of using attractiveness and expertise to endorse products/services. Endorsers reportedly are more effective when there is a match between the endorser and the endorsed product.

Maturation
This is the stage in a well-known product/service's life cycle where sales are stable.

Mean
The mean is the average of the observed numbers calculated by adding up all the numbers and then dividing them by how many numbers there are; i.e., it is the sum of all the observations divided by the count.

Means-ends chain analysis
A method to help us understand how our consumer values match features/benefits in products and services.

Measurement protocol (Google Analytics)
This is a feature of Google Analytics (GA) that has the ability to send data directly to Google Analytics servers (and thus to a website's GA accounts). It also measures how users interact with a business from any environment (and not just the website), for example it:

- Measures the users activity in new environments
- Ties online to offline behaviour
- Sends data from both client and server.

Media review
A review of video and audio content to ensure they include captions, audio descriptions and transcripts where appropriate to ensure the content they contain is accessible.

Medium
In Google Analytics, this is used to identify the origin of referral to a website alongside Source. Medium generally refers to the channel type of the referral — for example organic, PPC (paid search), referral, email, or none for direct traffic.

Megamenu
A dropdown menu with a lot of content. *See also Dropdown label/menu.*

M

Memorability
The degree to which users can remember how to use an interface.

Mental (psychological) accounting
This is how people code, categorise and evaluate the economic outcomes of their buying behaviour. And, they may have multiple mental accounts for the same kind of money resource. For example, a person may use different monthly budgets for their groceries and for eating out/ takeaways. They may also restrict certain kinds of purchase when their budget has run out, whereas they may continue buying other things even when they have to be paid for from the same source. You can see this when people pay for goods in a supermarket using cash. The tendency is to spend less money when paying in cash, while they will spend more using a debit/ credit card although the payments are coming out of the same resource.

Mental workload
The more mental effort required to complete a website task, the more likely it is to cause friction for visitors. Eye tracking can be used to observe pupil diameter in measuring mental workload. The greater the demand, the larger the pupil becomes (but under rare and extreme circumstances pupils will constrict) and vice versa. *See also Eye tracking.*

Mere exposure effect
Refers to how people can develop a preference for familiar things. It is also known as the familiarity principle.

Message match
It is important that advertising and emails match website messages. Visitors should not be confused when they arrive at a website and find out it is not what they expected to see.

Meta tag
Text snippets that describe a webpage's content that appear only in the webpage's code.

Metrics
Specific measurement of something. On a website this is a quantitative measurement of statistics that describe events or activities.

In UX there are specific measurements used to evaluate the effectiveness of the experience such as the number of pages viewed or number of visitors to the experience.

Raw metrics can be categorised into two broad groups: counts and measures (or as discrete and continuous data).

1 Counts — how many — a count or tally of the number of particular items, e.g., users, page views
2 Measures — how much — the size or capacity of something, e.g., time on website.

In reporting and analytics, it is often discussed which metrics are effectively calculated metrics based on different counts or measures. For example, an ecommerce rate is the count of sales expressed as a percentage of the count of sessions.

Micro conversion
Activities frequently completed by users on a website prior to completing the main conversion goal (macro conversion). For example, activities such as a newsletter signup, adding a product to basket, or account creation often precede a purchase.

Microcopy
Microcopy refers to the essential words used to:

- Label form fields
- Clarify the purpose of a button
- Provide instructions

- Request a delivery address and explain delivery options
- Explain payment options
- Provide error messages
- Reassure the checkout is secure
- Offer a guarantee, etc.

All the above help visitors move efficiently from point of entry to a website and through the checkout. It's important not to use microcopy to prop up poor design and layout.

Microsite
A small website dedicated to a specific marketing campaign. It can be an individual webpage or a small cluster of webpages that function as a discrete website, but within an existing website. A microsite can have its own domain name or a subdomain.

Millennials
Those who reached adulthood in the early 2000s. *See also Generation Y.*

Minesweeping
An action designed to identify where on a page links are located. Minesweeping involves the user rapidly moving the cursor or pointer over a webpage, watching to see where the cursor or pointer changes to indicate the presence of a link. *See also Mouseover.*

Miscomprehension
Incorrect understanding (wrong idea) of what people see, hear, etc.

Motivated reasoning
Emotion-biased decision-making by consumers that allows them to reach a desired conclusion.

Mobile
A device. And the most important device for ecommerce.

Ecommerce companies need to factor in mobile shopping within their strategy according to IMRG:

"Shoppers using mobile devices account for over 45 per cent of all ecommerce traffic in the UK."

Sales made via a smartphone grow 97 per cent year-on-year.

Mobile first
The practice of designing websites and writing content for mobile devices as the primary goal, with desktop as secondary. Needs careful application as there are obvious differences in the technology and implications for visitors/customers.

Modal/non-modal or modality
A webpage or window that forces the user's interaction.

Moderated user testing
Website user testing that involves a moderator who is at hand to monitor test participants and oversee the session. These tests enable maximum, meaningful data capture and if the test takes place in a usability lab it can be watched discretely by other conversion optimisers in an observation room. From there, the other observers can feedback to the moderator about what they are seeing. The data collection capabilities from effectively run moderated tests are far reaching, and the insights can be extremely valuable. *See also Unmoderated user testing, Boomerang, Echoing and Columbo.*

Modular design system
This relies on the creation of templates or standardised page types that are populated with reusable, standardised content modules. Modules allow for reuse across the experience and also standardise the look and feel of content.

Moments of truth

These are crossroad moments during a customer's long-term relationship with a company or brand. Whatever happens at this point could cause the customer to abandon or encourage them to continue to do business with a brand.

Mood board

A collage, either physical or digital, which is intended to communicate the visual style a direction is heading.

Moral tax of paying

Every payment made has a moral tax of consumption. Its magnitude is influenced by how buyers pay and when they pay.

Motion

Moving webpage elements such as parallax scrolling can attract attention. However, care should be taken in applying motion as it could overwhelm website visitors, become a distraction, and a point of friction that will detract from the objective of the webpage.

Motivation

Reason(s) for people's actions, desires and needs; how they set and achieve a goal.

Motor cortex

The motor cortex is the part of the frontal cortex involved in planning, controlling, and performing voluntary movement.

Mouse tracking

The use of software to collect a website visitor's mouse cursor positions on a webpage. It is important to note that it does not represent what the visitor is looking at. Only eye tracking can provide an accurate picture of what the visitor looks at.

Mouseover

A graphical control element that is activated when the user moves or hovers

the pointer over the trigger area using a mouse or a digital pen.

Multichannel

Experience or activity that is rendered in more than one channel. For example, a website that can be accessed on mobile phones, tablets, and desktops together with physical stores, catalogue sales and direct sales. The idea is to give customers choice and convenience, which improves relationships and loyalty.

Multichannel ecommerce

Selling goods/services across different channels and devices.

Multi-Channel Funnels

A series of Google Analytics reports that look at the interaction of tracked traffic types to conversions. They include assisted conversion, top conversion path, time lag and path length reports.

Multi-step forms

These aim to reduce friction by splitting long forms into several steps, making it easier for the user to complete as a series of smaller tasks. For example, if a form has 20 or more fields, splitting the fields over four separate pages with progress bars can increase the completion rate of the form. *See also Self-efficacy.*

Multivariate testing

This is the process of testing multiple combinations of a webpage's elements at the same time to identify which combination delivers the highest conversion rate.

Myers-Briggs Type Indicator (MBIT)

A framework for describing behavioural styles based on cognitive predispositions.

N

N

Narrative style

Writing chronologically by beginning with an introduction and finishing with a conclusion isn't appropriate for the web. Website visitors scan for key information so use the inverted pyramid technique instead. *See also Inverted pyramid.*

Navigation

Navigation plays a crucial role in getting website visitors to view more than just the home page and help them do what they want to do. A key thing about navigation is that it must work and must not provide a source of friction. It has various formats such as global navigation, breadcrumb trails, related links, pagination, footer. Navigation is generally represented visually by buttons, forward and back arrows, tabs, and hyperlinked text. It's important that any (pathway) webpages that the visitor is taken to must help get them to where they want/need to be quickly and efficiently. *See also Pathway pages.*

Need for cognition

How much people like to think; i.e., how inclined they are towards effortful cognitive activities.

Need for uniqueness

The pursuit of differentness relative to others that is achieved through buying, using and disposing of goods/services for the purpose of developing and enhancing personal and social identities.

Need recognition

When people experience recognition of their current state and the state they desire.

Needfinding/need finding

Talking to website visitors/customer to discover their needs — those they might explicitly state, and those hidden beneath the surface. Understanding the audience provides meaningful insights to inspire and inform a final, impactful design.

Needs

Necessities whether actual or perceived.

Negative interactions

The effect of two or more input variables combining to produce a noticeably worse outcome than predicted by the settings of the individual variables.

Negative keyword

Keywords used to prevent an advert from being triggered by a certain word or phrase. It tells Google not to show an advert to anyone who searches using that word (phrase).

Negative word-of-mouth communication

Negativity shared about a product or service to other consumers.

Neocortex (neopallium/isocortex/new brain)

The largest part of the brain (the grey matter) and about 85 per cent of the human brain's total mass. It is concerned with higher mental functioning (and sight and hearing). It is thought to be the most recently evolved part of the cerebral cortex.

Net promoter score

A metric that gauges the loyalty of customers and determines the likelihood of them recommending a product or service to others.

Neural pathway

Connected neurons that activate in sequence to produce a specific function.

Neuron

A specialised cell (nerve cell) that processes and transmits information through our central nervous system using electrical and chemical signals. The brain is said to contain 100 billion neurons.

Neuronal circuit

A neuronal circuit carries information from one point in the body or nervous system to another along a functional pathway formed of neurons. It can have both feed back and feed forward loops and it uses electrical and chemical energy to transmit the information.

Neuromarketing

Marketing research into consumers' sensorimotor, cognitive, and affective responses to marketing stimuli. Researchers investigate such things as changes in the brain, heart rate, respiratory rate and electrodermal activity.

Neurotransmitter

Chemicals that communicate information throughout the brain and body. They carry information across the space between a neuron's nerve terminal and another neuron's dendrites.

New versus returning metrics and reporting

Reports that look at the difference in site performance between a first time and repeat experience of a website. Often referred to with regards to users, sessions or at a customer level (for first time versus repeat purchasing behaviour). Due to the nature of website tracking this is not always a perfect representation because it is limited by what can be identified accurately.

New sessions percentage

The estimated overall percentage of first time visits to a website.

New users percentage

The percentage of first time users on a website in a specified period.

Next generation text service

This is a telephony service that uses text messaging to enable businesses to communicate with customers who are unable to hear or speak.

Noncomparable decisions

Making choices about products or services from different categories.

Noncompensatory model

When negative information leads to the rejection of a product/service. Therefore, people make noncompensatory choices by considering attributes sequentially and recognising the benefits of some attributes may not overbalance shortfalls on others.

Nonmarketer dominated source

An influential source external to the vendor; for example, colleagues, friends, family, TV, etc.

Nonparametric

A type of multivariate testing data analysis that tries to identify the best performing recipe in the landing page search space without building a model involving the input variables. *See also (and contrast with) Parametric.*

Normal distribution

This is an arrangement of a data set where the majority of the values cluster in the middle of the range and the rest taper off symmetrically toward either extreme. This arrangement is generally represented graphically by a bell curve chart. *See also Bell curve.*

Normative choice tactics

Low effort decision making that uses other people's opinions. For example, buying a similar product to a friend, wearing a pair of socks that were a gift, etc.

Normative influences

How people conform to the beliefs/standards of a group.

Norms

Standards typical to a group or thing.

N

Noticeability

The visibility of an area on a website can be measured using eye tracking. This will provide a measure of how many people noticed it and how quickly they noticed it. *See also Eye tracking.*

Nucleus accumbens

An area of the brain found in the basal forebrain. This area experiences increases in dopamine levels as a result of rewarding.

Null hypothesis

The hypothesis that A/B testing aims to disprove is a null hypothesis. The null hypothesis states that the conversion rates of control and variants are the same (or not significantly different).

Numbered lists

A list where individual items are numbered. Use these on forms to indicate the systematic steps needed to set up an account, etc. The numbers also give instant indication of how many steps there are and can check each one off as they complete each one.

NUX

New user experience.

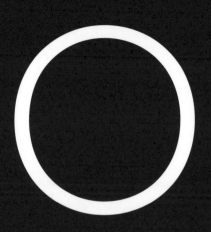

Objective comprehension
The level of understanding of a marketing message/argument.

Observation room
A room located away from the usability laboratory where tests and test participants can be viewed and further monitored discretely.

Occam's (Ockham's) Razor
The most effective (and perhaps most reliable) explanations and theories employ minimal assumptions. The figurative razor shaves away unnecessary or unsubstantiated aspects of a written or spoken theory or explanation.

Occipital lobe
The caudal/posterior part of the cerebral cortex responsible for vision and visual recognition of objects and faces.

Offer/offering
A product, service, activity or idea, which is the focus of the sales copy on a website.

Offline conversions
A conversion that doesn't happen on a website itself. This might be a conversion that happens on the phone in a call centre or even a physical transaction of some kind in store, but it is important to consider offline conversions if they are potentially driven by online activity.

Omnichannel
Omnichannel (omni-channel) refers to using multiple sales channels that aim to provide customers with a seamless shopping experience whether they are shopping online from a desktop or mobile device, by telephone or in a physical store.

On demand
Delivering a service or giving access to software over the Internet as and when required by the customer. *See also Cloud computing and SaaS.*

One-sided message
Advertising that only presents the positive information available.

One-tailed test (or one-sided test)
Also called a directional test or hypothesis, a one-tailed test is a test of significance of a relationship between two variables in only one specific direction and ignoring the possibility of a relationship in the opposite direction.

For example, in an experiment the test would be to discover whether the treatment had a positive outcome (e.g., conversion rate improvement), and ignoring the possibility that it was negative.

In effect, this provides more power to detect an effect because the overall significance level is not being split in two. For example, a 5 per cent significance level in a one-tailed test is the equivalent of 10 per cent in a two tailed test, and, as such, a one tailed test shouldn't just be chosen to report a significant effect.

Ongoing search
Regular searching that may or may not lead to a decision.

Online customer surveys
These assist with identifying the primary audience of a website. They help with gathering information about what visitors needs are, what concerns them, and what causes friction for them while using the website. *See also Survey.*

Online processing
What people do while viewing an advert or a promotion.

Open ended questions
Questions with no right or wrong or finite answer. Used in customer surveys and polls to give users freedom to reply in any way. Useful in qualitative research to gain unexpected information.

Open rate

When using email marketing, the open rate can be calculated by dividing the number of email messages opened by the total number of email messages sent (excluding those that bounced) and then expressed as a percentage. Services such as MailChimp provide tracking reports that show open rates and allow you to A/B test to improve them.

Open source software

Open source software is developed by and for the user community. It usually involves collaborative development from multiple independent sources.

Operant conditioning

Behaviour based on what someone has learnt or been subjected to in the past. It is a process that attempts to modify behaviour through the use of positive and negative reinforcement. It's how associations are made between a particular behaviour and its consequence.

Opinion

Opinions are of little value in optimisation. Decisions need to be based on testing and data. The nearest thing to an acceptable opinion being raised is during heuristic analysis where an expert may spot something that is not normal such as the positioning of navigation bars, logos, etc.

Opinion leader

A person that has the ability to influence the decisions of many.

Optic chiasm(a)

This is where parts of each optic nerve from the left and right eyes form an X-shaped structure. It allows the visual cortex to receive the same hemispheric visual field from both eyes.

Optic nerve

The nerve connecting the retina in the eye to the brain.

Opt-in

Choosing to participate. It should be explained clearly what subscribers will receive in return for exchanging their contact details.

Optimal stimulation level

This is contextual and refers to the most appropriate amount of motivation needed to make a decision. So, it will vary from situation to situation.

Optimisation

The process of improving.

Optimise

To make a webpage, form or website function/feature as effective as possible through testing and data analysis.

Order value

The revenue value of an ecommerce transaction. *See also Average order value.*

Organic traffic

Website traffic defined coming directly from an unpaid search engine listing.

Outbound links

Links that direct website visitors to other websites.

Outcome expectancies

People like to know what to expect as an outcome of doing something. So, it's a good idea to tell customers in advance what will happen, for example, *"Click here to see your free quote".*

Outlier

User test observations that are abnormally far from the rest of the collected values. If outliers are included, errors can be introduced.

Output variables

The things that are measured in an experiment. The objective is to find out how changing the input variables will change the output variables (e.g., conversion rate, revenue and profit per visitor).

Outsource
Hiring a third party organisation to look after certain business functions such as conversion optimisation, web design, logistics, fulfilment, etc. Outsourcing enables ecommerce companies to concentrate on the business of selling.

Over recruiting (eye tracking experiments)
It is advisable to recruit more participants than the minimum requirement for the test because some participants will not calibrate or track well enough to produce meaningful data.

Overlapping AOIs
Describes how two (or more) areas of interest (AOIs) intersect. This overlapping can present problems for the website visitor and they cause difficulties when trying to measure fixations with eye tracking. For example, there is a danger of double counting, leading to overestimating the amount of attention given to the overlapping AOIs.

P

Padding
The margin around a button, etc.

Page comp
A design tool that captures a visual illustration of a page or template, showing the look and feel of the page. It shows what visual elements fall on a page (images, photos, colours and typography), where the elements are placed, and what size and shape each element is.

Page density
A measure of the percentage of the screen that is filled with text and graphics.

Page depth
This is a measurement of the number of pages on a website that a visitor views during a single browser session. *See also Depth of visit.*

Page flow
A hierarchy or sequence suggested by arrangement of elements on a page.

Page templates
Predefined layouts or formats for sets of common webpages.

Page title
Page titles refer to the text located in the browser title bar (this is the bar found at the very top of the screen of common browsers).

Page views
A page view refers to each time a visitor views a page on a website. It is not a record of how many hits are generated.

Pain points
Points in UX that cause difficulties for website visitors/customers.

Palette
The selection of colours that are used for a design. A consistent palette is important for a cohesive design.

Panel data
Dataset in which the behaviour of entities is observed over time — used in statistics and econometrics. The analysis of data collected over long periods of time for the same individuals, groups, companies, etc., to understand changes over time.

Paper prototyping
A prototyping method in which paper models are used to simulate computer or web applications.

Parent product
A configurable product that can be customised by the customer. The customised version that the customer buys is known as a child product.

Parallax scrolling
Website graphic technique where a background image moves at a different speed to the foreground content when a visitor scrolls down a webpage.

Parallel design
A design methodology that involves several designers pursuing the same effort simultaneously, but independently, with the intention to combine the best aspects of each for the ultimate solution.

Parametric
A type of multivariate testing data analysis that attempts to build a model based on the input variables and their combinations to predict the corresponding value of the output variables. *See also Input Variables, Output Variables; contrast with Nonparametric.*

Parrot technique
A technique used in moderated user testing in which the moderator repeats the last phrase or word the user said, while using a slight questioning tone, in order to encourage the user to elaborate on what they said without leading them.

P

For example, User – "This form is odd", Moderator – "The form is odd?". *See also Echoing technique and Moderated user testing.*

Participatory design

An approach to design where those who will use the experience are invited to participate during the early stages of the design process to weigh in on how the design should function.

Passive incidental learning

Non conscious effort (low-energy) learning by absorbing information through repetition.

Passive space

Open areas outside of the main content areas, e.g., margins.

Password fields

The default for a user to sign up for something is for them to complete two password fields, one for entering their password and one for them to confirm it. However, this is unnecessary and causes friction. Removing the confirmation field and including a "show password" option so that the user self-validates their password will get rid of the friction.

Path

The route taken by a user as they move through a website. The path can be shown by breadcrumbs.

Path analysis

The analysis of user journeys through a website — illustrated in Google Analytics with flow reports. Also a term used in statistics to describe the direction of dependencies between variables.

Path to purchase

The customer's journey from awareness to purchase. It is a subset of the customer journey that focuses on the most direct route taken by a customer to get to making a purchasing decision.

Pathway

Indicates the user journey that represents the visitor's/customer's information needs. Pathways meld the business or organisational needs by creating a journey that will give them what they need to accomplish a task.

Pathway pages

Those webpages that help website visitors get to where they need to be. For example, they may search for a product on a website and the next webpage they go to will offer them a range of products/services similar to what they are searching for. The products will have a photo and a short one-line description. They should be able to scan/skim read the list and choose what looks suitable and then be taken to the next pathway page, which will have more detail, photographs, reviews, etc., and if they like it they can select it for purchase, and so on. This needs to provide a smooth transition through to checkout. *See also Navigation.*

Payment gateway

An ecommerce service that authorises card payments for online purchases.

PayPal

A payment processor/method owned by eBay and very popular with consumers. It can be included on websites as a payment option.

PDF

A file format used to present and exchange documents reliably and is compatible across different operating systems and hardware.

Peer review

When several colleagues review website copy and consideration is given to implementing their recommendations.

P

The revised version should be tested before making it live.

Perceived risk

This is the uncertainty a customer feels when buying a new product or signing up for a new service. They inevitably feel some doubts over whether what they buy will be fit for purpose, these fears are heightened if it is an expensive item. To help consumers overcome perceived risk, statements like "100 per cent satisfaction guaranteed or your money back" can trigger them to buy. See also Triggers.

Perception

An active constructive process of interpreting and organising sensations.

Perception related failure

When an incorrect webpage element is selected. Caused by such things as poor placement and presentation of the target, lack of relevancy, unusual/unpredictable appearance or competing elements that are easily mistaken for the target.

Perceptual organisation

How sensory stimuli are organised into groups.

Perceptual process

This is a sequence of psychological steps taken when organising and interpreting information from a sensation. The sequence is:

- Observation
- Perception to select objects
- Organising our perception of objects
- Interpreting perceptions
- Response.

See also Sensation.

Performance

How fast the website loads across different connections and how it copes when inundated with users. Also, the measure of whether a product/service fulfils our needs.

Performance risk

Whether a product/service will perform as expected.

Performance related tactics

Selecting a product/service by benefits, features or evaluations by others.

Peripheral route processing

Low-energy/effort evaluation of a message based on physical attractiveness, background music, or other surface-level characteristics rather than the actual content of the message.

Peripheral route to persuasion

Using other stimuli to help buyers decide in addition to the main marketing message. This could be hearing an influencer make positive comments, for example.

Permission marketing

Delivering anticipated, personal and relevant messages to people who expect to receive them.

Persistent cart

This is a useful feature used by ecommerce websites that remembers customers' items whether they continue on a website or leave without buying. The customer can return later to find what they'd already selected still in the cart and continue shopping/buying.

Persistent cookies

These are cookies that stay on a computer until they are either deleted manually or because they have reached their set expiration data. Using these, it is possible to maintain information about on-site behaviour and activity over time beyond that of session cookies. See also Session cookies.

P

Persistent navigation (global navigation)

Navigation that appears on every page of a website.

Persona

A fictional customer who resembles an ideal customer. Using website data, personas can be created to represent customers for each segment of a business (and that includes the devices they use for online shopping). So, rather than thinking generically about customers/potential customers, content can be developed to align with all the different personas. *See also Cohort.*

Personal relevance

What people see as important to them in a product/service — therefore how they link their needs, goals, and values and product knowledge.

Personalisation

Customised website content that aims to match the interest of individual visitors; showing them relevant products/services or information that best suits their interests.

Personality

Personal characteristics that determine how we behave in various situations.

Websites have personalities too. These are established and supported by the design, colour, graphics, typography, content, writing style and words. The personality needs to align with the website visitor audience and their expectations.

Persuasion

American psychologist Robert Cialdini offers seven principles of persuasion. These are:

- Reciprocity (give something to get something back)
- Social proof (people will do things that they see other people are doing)
- Commitment/consistency (when people commit to an idea or goal, they are more likely to honour their commitment)
- Authority (people tend to obey authority figures)
- Liking (people are easily persuaded by other people that they like)
- Scarcity (perceived scarcity generates a demand)
- Unity (when people perceive others to be the same as them, they will be influenced by them also).

Phone interview

A semi-structured or structured interview that is conducted by telephone or other voice technology (e.g., Skype).

Photographs

Visual elements on a website. Other than product photographs for conveying factual information, photographs can create emotional connections with the target audience.

Phrase match

Google AdWords keyword setting that only allows an advert to show when someone searches using a specified phrase (or a close match) with words either side of it. For example: "red shoes" would potentially show an ad for the search queries "buy red shoes" or "red shoes in size 10" but not "red mens shoes".

Physical consistency

Refers to the "look and feel" of a website. Physically consistent webpages will have logos, headers, and navigation elements all located in the same place. The pages also will use the same fonts and graphic elements across all webpages in the website.

Physical detachment

People's mindset when they get rid of something.

P

Pingdom

A service that tracks the uptime, downtime, and performance of websites.

Pinterest

A content curation platform that allows users to organise and share interesting content that they find on the web, that they upload themselves or that they see with other users. It is a social networking site, a pinboard, a gift finder, a wish list and a tool for collaboration all in one.

Placement

This refers to arranging form fields that go together, closer to each other. Even subtle adjustments in placement can make a big difference.

Plain language

Make it easier for visitors to use a website by using plain language. Use familiar words, short sentences, helpful headings that offer guidance, and avoid using jargon.

Plug-in

A software module that adds a specific feature or service to a larger system. For example, there are a number of plug-ins for common browsers that enable them to display different types of audio and video.

PNG

A raster graphics file format that supports lossless data compression and is used commonly by websites. It's good for images with large areas of uniform colour or those with transparent backgrounds.

Polls

Performing a website poll enables the collection of qualitative data. It helps with providing information about why customers do what they do, the choices they make, what helped them to decide, are there any improvements that can be done to improve the customer experience.

Polymath

A person whose expertise spans a significant number of different subject areas.

Point-and-click

A term used to describe conventional web surfing behaviour. When a user visually identifies a link they wish to follow, they place their mouse pointer over the link (point) and depress the appropriate button on the mouse (click). *See also Mouseover.*

Popups

A form of web advertising designed to disrupt the user and grab their attention. They are often used to capture email addresses (e.g., offering a discount off a purchase for their email address) or as an upsell (e.g., offering complimentary products they may like) after they have added a product to the basket. *See also Jarrett-Zetie rules of popups.*

Portal

The part of a website dedicated to customers enabling them to log-in to view accounts, access services, etc.

Positive interactions

The effect of two or more input variables combining to produce a noticeably better outcome than predicted by the settings of the individual variables.

Positive mimicry

This is where people compare their own behaviour to others. Websites can employ strategies such as showing how customers use your website/products/services through social media posts and forums. Also, displaying the most popular products that customers buy, showing what people search for and eventually buy, and rewarding customers for positive interactions encourages positive mimicry.

P

Possession rituals

The things people do after buying something to make it their own.

Post conversion

Achieving a sale is not the end of the relationship with a customer. Websites should build on it to make future sales. For example, use the confirmation page/email to promote and educate them about other offers, services, etc.

Post decision dissonance

Anxiety over whether the correct purchasing decision has been made.

Post decision rationalisation/ post purchase rationalisation

People develop reasons for why they've bought something. It occurs (to varying degrees) when they buy a high-value item like a mobile phone, for example. Because people don't often want to feel like they have made the wrong decision they will seek to rationalise their decision by preferring to acknowledge and focus on the weaknesses of alternatives and the strength of the product that has been chosen. This rationalisation process allows consciousness to reassure that the right decision has been made. But these reasons can be unreliable, so researchers/marketers need to be aware of this when conducting surveys.

Post hoc analysis

To review the data after an experiment has concluded.

PPC (pay-per-click)

Internet advertising method used to direct traffic to websites; the advertiser pays a publisher when their ad is clicked. There are various advertising outlets from online publications to search engines, with Google AdWords being the most well-known.

PR

Public relations (PR) refers to the process of assisting the building and maintaining of a brand's reputation by communicating with the general public and its target market(s).

Preattentive processing

Subconscious processing of stimuli received by a person's peripheral vision. Visual stimuli that can be processed in less than 250 milliseconds are, therefore, considered preattentive. Understanding and taking advantage of preattentive processing improves intuitiveness and yield a faster and more natural user experience for website visitors and customers.

Precision

The level of accuracy in sampling and consistency in repeated sampling.

Predictive analytics

This is an area of data mining concerned with extracting information from data to use it to predict trends and behaviours. It is a technique that is being used increasingly in ecommerce to understand customer behaviour and tailor a number of factors from pricing, stock, customer servicing and promotions.

Preference marketing

Tracking of a person's online activities over time, including their searches, their webpage visits, and content they view to target their interests with appropriate advertising and messages. *See also Behavioural targeting.*

Prepurchase search

The stage in a consumer's decision-making process where they seek information to help them decide what kind of products or which specific product will fulfil their need(s).

P

P

Present-focus bias

This refers to how people appreciate early rewards, and the sooner they receive them, the higher they are valued — and, so, they are more likely to buy things that appeal to their present-focus bias that provide such early, high-value rewards.

Price anchoring

Makes other options look less expensive on a pricing table, by using a more expensive product or service as a comparison. See also Anchoring.

Pricing

Setting the price of a product. In addition to the price of the product, clearly indicate to customers when an extra cost has been added or updated, and if possible give them control over the additional cost (for example, shipping costs). Likewise, always display the total cost as soon as possible, preferably before the user has invested a significant amount of time going through the checkout or handing over their email address.

Primacy effect

The first stimuli presented in a series are remembered better or more easily.

Primary data

Data collected directly by a researcher/the research team.

Primary reference group

The group that researchers interact with directly.

Priming

Exposing website visitors/customers or test participants to stimuli designed to encourage them to take action.

Privacy

The right of website visitors/customers to be free from intrusion and free from unauthorised disclosure of their personal data or information. Websites need to be fully aware of — and uphold and respect — privacy. This can be displayed in a website privacy policy together with an explanation of what the company will do with the information it needs to collect and store to fulfil customer orders/subscriptions.

Probability distribution function

In probability distribution theory, the probability distribution function describes the set of possible outcomes for an event along with their likelihood. Also called a probability density function.

Probability theory

Mathematics that is concerned with describing and analysing random events.

Probing

Follow up questioning to clarify why an earlier response was given.

Procedural memory

Memory that allows people to perform skills based on what has been learned: making a cup of tea, brushing teeth, riding a bike, etc. Because they involve an action or actions, they are more likely to be remembered.

Process

A series of actions or steps taken in order to achieve a particular end. Conversion optimisation is process driven. There are systematic steps needed to enable an optimisation project to proceed.

Product image

What people think about the attributes of a brand's product(s). They can be perceived or real, and conveyed through communications, packaging, or personal experience.

Product pictures

Product pictures are often part of the pathway through a website. Remember to include some details about the product to help. The information should reflect the website visitor's initial questions about the product, for example, product name, price, colour and size availability, and customer ratings.

Product series
People like to collect and complete sets of products. Websites can tap into this by grouping certain products within their ranges to encourage people to collect them. They can also show what other products go with the one they are buying.

Production stage
The stage at which the high-fidelity design is fleshed out, content and digital assets are created, and a high-fidelity version of the product is validated by stakeholders and end-users through user testing sessions. The role of the user experience (UX) designer then shifts from creating and validating ideas, to collaborating with developers to guide and champion the vision.

Profit
Money earned after paying expenses, costs and taxes. Profit = total revenue minus total business expenses.

Promo code
Abbreviation for promotional code, which allows the person presenting the code to get discounts or special deals not available to the general public.

Progress indicator
A progress indicator helps with form filling. It informs customers exactly where they are in registration/subscription/check out process and encourages them to continue and complete their task.

Progress principle
The progress principle states that more happiness is derived from making progress towards goals than from achieving them.

Progressive disclosure
An interactive design technique that helps maintain the focus of a user's attention by reducing clutter, confusion, and cognitive workload. It improves usability by presenting only the minimum data required for the task at hand.

Progressive enhancement
Web design strategy for creating websites that are accessible to all devices, using a layered approach. It emphasises accessibility, semantic HTML markup (e.g., <form>, <table>, and <img>), and external stylesheet (CSS) and scripting technologies.

Project kick-off
The formally recognised start of a project.

Proofreading
Checking for spelling errors by reading from the bottom of the copy to the top. This stops the proofreader from reading for sense and checking for grammatical errors, enabling them to focus on each word instead. Then they read through the copy again from top to bottom checking for grammatical errors.

Prototype
A rough guide for the layout of a website or app that indicates the direction the product is heading. *See also Low-fidelity prototype.*

Proximity
The placement of elements in relation to each other in a composition. Elements that are close together are perceived to be more related than those that are more widely spaced apart.

Psychographics
Consumers' personality, values, opinions, attitudes, interests, and lifestyles. Understanding these characteristics helps to understand why they buy.

P

Psychographic segmentation
Segmentation of an audience based upon psychographic characteristics.

Psychology
Psychology is the study (both academic and applied) of behaviour. It covers all aspects of conscious and unconscious experience as well as thought.

Pull quote
A short quote or excerpt pulled from the main text and used as a visual element to help highlight important ideas and draw interest to the piece.

Pupil centre corneal reflection (PCCR)
A technique used by eye trackers to model eye and gaze position and also enables a calculation of pupil size. It uses cameras to capture the reflection of light on the cornea and in the pupil of the eye and then performs numerous calculations on this data to model the eye accurately.

Pupil dilation
An emotional response measure. *See also Dilation.*

P-value
A p-value is a probability associated with a test statistic. It is the probability of obtaining at least as strong/extreme results given that the null hypothesis (H_0) is true. In all conversion optimisation experiments there will (or should) be an observable effect or difference between the groups being tested. For example, if a webpage was shown to 1000 people and exactly the same page was shown to another 1000 people, it is unlikely that the conversion rates would be exactly the same because there would be variability across the samples. However, you wouldn't expect the variation to be drastically high or low. This variability provides the p-value, which, if it is high, leads to rejecting the null hypothesis, and if low, accepting it.

P

Q

QA (quality assurance)

QA is a set of processes, standards and policies that are put in place to ensure products and services are developed in the correct way.

QC (quality control)

The process of ensuring the product or service behaves in the way it is expected to.

Quantitative and qualitative research

Quantitative research helps to discover what actually happens and qualitative research helps with finding out why things happen and how many times they happen.

Query

A filtered request from a database.

Query string

A filtered request from a database contained in the URL of a webpage.

Questionnaires

A research instrument consisting of a series of questions and other prompts for the purpose of gathering information from respondents.

Quirks mode

In webpages, an incomplete, missing or outdated DOCTYPE puts web browsers into quirks mode. The browser assumes the markup and code is out-of-date and invalid. *See also DOCTYPE.*

R

Radio buttons

These enable users to self-select an appropriate option. Radio buttons work best when the choice is limited to less than five options.

 To be   Not to be

Random sample

A subset that is taken randomly from a larger group.

Random variable

A variable whose value varies due to chance. (Also known as a random quantity, aleatory variable or stochastic variable.)

Rate card

Indicates pricing for promotional advertising. Rate cards are commonly expressed in cost per thousand impressions.

Rational

Humans like to think of themselves as rational, i.e., having the ability to apply logic/reason to decisions/actions. But, humans are not rational. Instead, more often than not, they make a decision and then rationalise it after the event.

Reactance

Not conforming to what is expected to be done — and sometimes doing the complete opposite.

Readability

How easy it is for a person to read text. Website content should use the simplest language possible making it easy to understand for all. *See also Visual fluency*

Reading gravity

People scan across a webpage from left to right and then down to the bottom right-hand corner, which is known as reading gravity. *For further explanation, see also Gutenberg Diagram.*

Recall

How information is retrieved from the memory.

Recency

The length of time since a previous action. Used frequently in analytics reporting against visits but also can be applied to other metrics. *See also Frequency.*

Recency effect

A cognitive bias that causes people to prefer and react to new information/ experiences compared with older information/experiences. For example, latter items in a list are recalled better than those at the beginning. This goes for marketing messages too. But, that does not mean that new is always better.

Receptor

An end organ (or a group of end organs) in sensory or afferent neurons that are sensitive to stimuli.

Recipe

In multivariate testing, a recipe is the unique combination of values for all the variables in the test.

Reciprocity

The practice of exchanging things with others for mutual benefit. For example, a user gives their email address in exchange for a discount on a purchase.

Recirculation

Repeated exposure to the same information. It helps with remembering without having to actively learn what is seen/heard.

Recognition

Determining whether someone has previously encountered a particular stimulus. Also, remembering words or situations.

R

Recurring events

This refers to repeating occurrences that develop a sense of belonging, anticipation and sustained interest. Letting customers know about period discounts and updating them about new products/services are examples of recurring events that may encourage them to keep coming back to a website.

Redirects

The process by which a URL takes a user to an alternative webpage without them taking any action. There are different types of redirect used for differing purposes and commonly for search engine optimisation (e.g., 301 redirects are referred to as permanent redirects, 302 are temporary).

It is common to use redirects to manage a user's journey away from webpages which no longer exist on a website to more relevant and current pages.

Red route

Frequent and critical activities that visitors perform on a website. They are complete activities, not single tasks, and will probably use several webpages. Defining a website's red routes allows identification and elimination of any usability obstacles on important user journeys. (Important roads in London are known as "red routes" and Transport for London does everything in its power to make sure passenger journeys on red routes are completed as smoothly and quickly as possible.)

Reference group

Those people recognised to be similar to each other because of their values, position in society, work, etc.

Referral traffic

Used in analytics platforms such as Google Analytics to identify traffic to a website from other websites that are not from search results or otherwise tagged as specific campaign activity (see also Manual tagging). Reported in Google Analytics as a Medium with the site name as Source.

Reflective decision making

"... our conscious, reasoning self that has beliefs, makes choices, and decides what to think about what we do..." (Daniel Kahneman, 2007)

Reflective-Impulsive Model

The Reflective-Impulsive Model is the first dual process model that incorporates both System 1 and System 2. It explains social behaviour as a joint function of reflective and impulsive processes. Here two interacting systems, that operate differently from each other, control social behaviour.

The reflective system (System 2) uses facts and values to make behavioural decisions.

The impulsive system (System 1) causes behaviour by associative links (connections between memories) and motivational orientation that define a particular action.

SEE FIGURE 23

Reflexive evaluation

Feedback from others about a purchase or the intention to purchase something. It helps affirm thoughts about whether a person is doing/has done the right thing.

Refreshable Braille display

An electro-magnetic device that displays Braille characters via round tipped pins that are raised through holes in a flat surface.

Regression analysis

A statistical process for estimating the relationship between variables to understand the impact of the change in one on another. Widely used in forecasting potential results. There are a number of

R

different models and techniques (e.g., linear regression, simple regression, etc.).

Regression to the mean

Regression toward (or to) the mean is a statistical phenomenon that occurs when a variable is extreme on its first measurement and closer to the average on its second measurement. This phenomenon is also seen when a variable is extreme on its second measurement and closer to the average on its first.

Regular expressions (regex)

A regular expression is a special character string used to create a search pattern that can be used to match patterns in a data set. This is a more advanced version of using "wildcards" (*, ?, [], !, -, #, etc.) in searches. It is very useful in analytics platforms and data analysis in order to search and match to multiple items with one expression or conversely to limit matching. Used in reporting, goals etc. (Note, not all standard regular expressions work in the Google Analytics interface).

Relative advantage

Superior benefits of a product/service compared with others.

Relevancy

Top landing pages must be evaluated and assessed for their relevancy to the audience. This is particularly important if paid traffic is being driven to those pages. Assess relevancy by asking such questions as: if visitors come from external websites can they recognise that they are continuing on their scent trail, do headlines match page content, do the call to actions match the value of what customers will get, are the images relevant?

Remarketing

Following up with website visitors that expressed interest but didn't buy/sign up. Examples are the use of automated or triggered emails.

Reminders

People may need a trigger to motivate them to return to a website. Gentle reminders via emails, social networks, ads, newsletters, etc., will keep a website and its products/services in their memories.

Remote user testing

Remote usability testing is similar to conventional usability testing except that participants don't come to a laboratory – instead, the participant carries out the test from their own location e.g., home, office or a contextually relevant location for the specific test (such as the gym for a fitness app).

Participants are asked to carry out tasks on a website/app and their behaviour is observed using screen sharing/recording technology. *See also Unmoderated user testing.*

Reposition

Changing the brand (and/or market position) of a company.

Representativeness heuristic

People make judgments/estimations about a product/service by comparing it to the others within its category (including the category leader).

Reptilian brain

Reportedly, the oldest brain as described in the theory of the triune brain. This is instinctive and acts without thinking; it governs the heartbeat, breathing, temperature and balance. It contains the brainstem and the cerebellum. Marketers engage the reptilian part of the brain with headlines and visual imagery, the things that are noticed immediately when a webpage opens. It is this part of the brain that asks, *"Is this for me, and if so, what's in it for me?"*. It's most responsive at the beginning and at the end of an interaction. *See also Triune brain.*

R

Required field indicator

An indicator on a form that requires the user to provide specific information. When indicating required fields on forms ensure that they are marked clearly. The general convention is to use an asterisk — but also give an explanation such as "required" to ensure everyone understands that the information is not optional. Placing the "required" explanation near the top of the form and separate from the introduction is helpful too; avoid putting it at the bottom of the form as it may be missed, which could cause frustration. The explanation can also be read by screen readers. *See also Forms.*

Research (discovery) stage

Research is an essential first stage in conversion optimisation and is also known as "discovery of what matters". The aim is to find the problems, the scale of the problems, and their impact on website performance. *See also Discovery of what matters.*

Resistance

The refusal to accept/comply with something.

Resolution

Refers to the scale of improvements seen in a landing page test when a certain number of total conversions are sampled.

Response-efficacy

People tend to believe that if they take certain actions they'll avoid threats. For example, being vaccinated against flu will protect from the virus.

Response involvement

The level at which people respond to stimuli varies. Some stimuli require low involvement, while others require higher effort. It can also reflect external things like how much time people have available, how they're feeling, whether the decision they need to make needs much thought, etc.

Responsive web design

Responsive web design is an approach to creating websites that provide optimal viewing and user experience across a wide range of devices (from mobile phones to desktop computer monitors).

Results

Results from tests run in a controlled environment assist the identification of which elements on a website are important to website visitors/customers. Therefore, the results provide important information that is used to iterate the test further or implement a solution that can be applied across the website.

Retargeting

Displaying adverts, banners or email messages to website visitors about the things they browsed earlier but didn't buy.

Retina

Light sensitive tissue at the back of the eye. The eye's cornea and lens create an image on the retina and this is converted to chemical and electrical signals that trigger nerve impulses, which are relayed to the brain through the optic nerve.

Retinotopy

The mapping of visual input from the retina to neurons, especially those neurons within the visual stream.

Retrieval

The process of remembering.

Retrieval cue

A stimulus that causes/enables a person's ability to remember.

Return on Investment

Measurement of a campaign performance.

It is calculated by comparing what is put in (e.g. cost) versus what is received (e.g. revenue).

R

Returns policy

A statement on a website that informs the customer how to return unwanted or incorrect goods and obtain a refund. It will typically state how long the customer has to return the goods, where to return the goods to, and how they will be refunded (direct to their payment card/account, a credit note, etc.).

Returns rate

The number of products sold that are returned to the seller for refunds. A potentially important factor in profitability and calculating true ROI and profitability. Optimisation can also look to improve return rate through both onsite changes, and by improving the complete customer experience online and offline.

Revenue (REVs)

The amount of money that a company receives during a specific period, including discounts and deductions for returned goods. It is the top line (gross income) figure from which costs are subtracted to determine net income. Revenue is calculated by multiplying the price at which products/services are sold by the number of units or amount sold. Increasing revenue and profit is a primary goal of conversion optimisation.

Revenue per visitor (RPV)

The amount of money generated each time a customer visits a website. Calculate RVP by dividing the total revenue by the total number of visitors to the site. It can also be used to estimate the value of each additional visitor.

Reward

A persuasive technique that aims to encourage people to sign up or buy. This needn't be anything big and it could be something as simple as providing them with an order form as soon as they click to buy.

Reward system

The reward system is a process within the brain activated as a result of pleasurable experiences and is responsible for reinforcing behaviour. For example, eating food or engaging in any other pleasurable activity, which results in the release of dopamine within the brain.

RGB

RGB or red, green, blue is a colour model that is used for on-screen purposes. RGB is an additive colour, so when mixing colours, we begin with black and finish with white as more colour is added.

Rich media

Adverts on webpages that use different technologies like streaming video and apps that interact instantly with the visitor. Also, adverts that change when a mouse moves over them.

Ring model

The Ring Model was developed by Craig Sullivan to look at the layers or levels reached by website visitors. It focuses on depth of engagement, not pages viewed and helps with identifying the key loss steps. And, it helps locate where traffic flow is stuck and unable to get to the next level. The main benefit is helping with finding which layer of a website needs the most help.

Risk reversal

The concept of taking the risk of buying away from customers through offering money back guarantees, payment plans for large purchases, etc.

Roadmap

The plan of action based on what was learned in customer journey mapping. Findings and recommendations lead to initiatives for improvement that are prioritised into immediate, medium- and long-term actions.

R

Rod cells

Around 120 million photoreceptor cells called rods are found in the retina. They are sensitive to light and dark but not colour. *See also Cones.*

ROI

This is a measure of marketing success. Return on investment (ROI) calculates and assesses how much is put into a campaign vs. the gains from the activity.

Rokeach value survey

Developed by Milton Rokeach (1918–1988), a social psychologist. It measures instrumental (preferable modes of behaviour) and terminal (desirable end states of existence) values. Instrumental values help us with achieving terminal values.

Rollovers

A state change that involves one element being replaced by another upon the mouse going over it.

Run of network

Distribution of an online advertisement across the whole network of available websites for a particular advertising network.

Rule of thirds

A theory that says if an image is divided equally with two vertical and two horizontal lines, the areas where the lines intersect will become focal points of the image.

RVP (retrospective verbal protocol)

A procedure used in eye tracking tests. Participants recall their experience after completing the task. *See also CVP (concurrent verbal protocol).*

R

S

SaaS

Software as a Service (SaaS) enables hosted software to be distributed to customers over the Internet. *See also Cloud computing and On demand.*

Saccade

Natural rapid eye movements. This is the rapid movement of the eyes between two fixation points. Eyes move from one point to another three to four times a second. The brain suppresses the movement to prevent seeing blurred images. Saccades bring visual images to the fovea so that they are focussed on. This movement is picked up in eye tracking technologies and produces gaze plot visualisations. During eye tracking tests, visual information is extracted from fixations when the eyes are relatively motionless and focusing on something. *See also Foveal vision and Eye tracking.*

Saccade destination

This refers to where someone looks. It depends on what they are looking at, why and what for. It is based on combinations of bottom-up attention and top-down attention.

Salient attributes

The things that are recognised as being the most important at that particular time or in a particular context.

Same page links

Used to take people to the appropriate place and content within a page. For example, in FAQs the questions can be listed at the top as a contents section with each one linking to the answer further down the page. This makes it much easier for people to navigate through the FAQs.

Sample size

Refers to the number of individual pieces of data collected in a survey or from an experiment. It is an important feature of conversion optimisation studies where the goal is to draw inferences about a population from a sample.

Sampling

In Google Analytics, this is the practice of selecting a subset of data from a website's traffic and reporting based on that sample. It is used to speed up certain reports by restricting the volume of data queried in nonstandard reporting. Different versions of Google Analytics will have different levels of sampling.

Satisfaction

Feeling happy about a decision.

Satisficing

Website visitors/customers don't always choose the optimal choice because they are in a hurry, instead they may choose the most reasonable option or what simply appears good enough.

Saturated main effect

This parametric model considers main effects only. It assumes that there are no variable interactions.

Scan

Online people don't read content, they scan it. That goes for visually impaired people too, as they "scan" with their ears while listening to their screen readers.

Scanability

How easy it is to scan and understand a body of text.

Scarcity

Emphasising scarcity is a psychological technique to encourage visitors to buy from a website. People can be prone to thinking they'll miss out on an offer if they don't act quickly. If scarcity is going to be emphasised in the copy, it is important that what is being stated is authentic, otherwise it will damage credibility. *See also Credibility.*

S

Scenario

A narrative describing a day in the life of a consumer persona, and probably includes how a website or app fits into their lives.

Scent trail

The extent to which a person's attention can be kept on a particular task or desired outcome based upon the visual cues placed within a website. The objective is to help customers along their scent trail to the very point where they find what they came to find and then complete their task (e.g., complete a transaction/form).

Schema

An organised pattern of thought or behaviour that arranges categories of information and the relationships among them.

Scientific control

This is an experiment/observation designed to minimize the effects of variables other than a specific independent variable. Using scientific control makes results more reliable as it makes it possible to compare differences between control measurements and other measurements. It, therefore, provides a standard against which the other experiments can be judged.

Scope

A definition of the limits of a project or experimental study.

Screen reader

A software program used to allow reading of content and navigation of the screen using speech or Braille output. Used primarily by people who have visual impairment. JAWS, NVDA and ChromeVox are examples.

Screen resolution

This refers to the number of horizontal and vertical pixels on a display screen. The more pixels, the more information is visible to the website visitor without scrolling. Screen resolutions have a pixel count such as 1600 × 1200, which means 1600 horizontal pixels and 1200 vertical pixels. Screen resolution trends change regularly and so it is important to analyse the Google Analytics for a website to identify which screen resolutions are being used by the visitors. The website can then be optimised to work across those resolutions.

Screenful

The portion of a webpage that is visible on any given user's monitor or screen at any given point in time. The size of the screenful is determined by the user's monitor size, screen resolution settings, and the user's selected font size.

Scroll map

A scroll map shows how far down the page people are scrolling and it can help with determining where visitors abandon the page.

Search

Searchers are buyers. On most websites, people who perform a search convert better; sometimes significantly better.

Search box

A search box helps people to navigate quickly to what they are looking for, whether it is a product or information. Place the search box at the top of the page to make it easy to find. It will make life easier for people using screen readers if it is one of the first things they hear when using a website.

Search engine spiders

Automated computer programs that are part of search engines that retrieve and index webpages for later retrieval in response to queries. Also known as web crawlers.

S

Search space size

In a test, the search space size is the total number of distinct recipes. *See also Recipe.*

Searching by attribute

Comparing brands by their features and benefits.

Searching by brand

Collecting information on one brand before looking at another.

Secondary data

Data collected by other parties. *See also Primary data.*

Security

Online security is a big worry for many people. Besides making payments secure, inform your visitors that they can shop with confidence.

Section 508 (of The Rehabilitation Act, US)

Its purpose is to eliminate barriers in IT. It applies to all Federal Agencies that develop, procure, maintain or use electronic and information technology. Any company selling to the US Government must ensure their products and services comply with all of the 11 accessibility guidelines Section 508 describes that are currently based on WCAG 1.0.

Segmentation

The grouping of customers based on similar characteristics to gain a better understanding of their needs so that they can be given a more personalised experience. This is a complex area and can include a wide range of opportunities such as segmenting for traffic sources, previous interactions, customer lifecycle, customer value to the business, geography, device, browser and so on.

Select all test

A test that helps to identify elements on a webpage that are not keyboard accessible and is often used in conjunction with the tab key navigation test.

Selection effect

Wrongly assuming that a segment of the traffic accurately represents the total is known as a selection effect. It can occur when promotion acquired traffic hits a website, skewing the results.

Self-concept

The image people create of themselves. It's who they think they are/how important they think they are, based on their own values and values held by others that they take into consideration, whether positive or negative.

Self-consistency coherence

After taking a decision or an action, it is highly probable that all a person's future behaviour will match that past behaviour. This is because they need consistent views and behaviours.

Self-determination theory

A theory of personal motivation concerned with supporting natural or intrinsic tendencies to behave in effective and healthy ways. Self-determination can tell people what they shouldn't do and it can offer positive recommendations to inform what should be done.

Self-efficacy

People are more likely to perform actions when they believe they are relevant to them and that they can complete them.

S

S

Self-generation

Working out something for oneself. People prefer their own ideas and use information they generate through their own efforts.

Self-referencing

Considering a marketing message in context of experience and/or self-concept.

Self-serving bias

Because people are protective of their ego and need to maintain and enhance their self-esteem, they focus on strengths and past achievements, while rejecting negative feedback and overlooking faults and failures. They, therefore, see achievements as those things made possible because of their own strengths, whereas faults and failures tend to be classed as those things caused by outside forces/influences over which they have no (or limited) control.

Semantic memory

Part of a person's long-term memory responsible for general knowledge — those ideas, concepts and other information that accrue throughout their lives. So, semantic memory includes such as names for things (colours, music, etc.), classification of different activities (e.g., football is a sport, engineering is an occupation, etc.), pronunciation of words and letters, and so on.

Sensation

The brain takes in information through the sensory systems resulting in the experience of sensations: sight, sound, smell, taste and touch.

Sensory appeal

People remember things better when they have experienced them using several senses. Websites may struggle with sensory appeal because they mainly rely on visual techniques, but adding audio and video may help people to experience products/services better than just seeing product images and reading copy.

Sensory memory

Sensory experiences retained temporarily in a person's memory. It is the shortest-term element of memory.

SEO (search engine optimisation)

The process of improving a website ranking in search engines, which ultimately means there is a greater opportunity for people to find the website. Don't try to cheat the search engines by peppering webpages with keywords, but do include keywords in webpage titles, in the URL, headline, headings and appropriately in the copy. And, include content that other websites will link to.

Sequence segmenting

Segmenting customer data based on actions completed. For example, show users who did X, and then went on to purchase Y.

SERP (search engine results page)

The webpage that is generated by searching for a given phrase on Google or other search engines. SEO aims to move webpages higher up the SERPs.

Service design

Designing a product according to the needs of customers, so that it's user-friendly, competitive and relevant to them.

Service level agreement

A contract between an external or internal service provider and a customer that explains the level of service they will provide. Often referred to as an SLA, the contract should be very specific about what the service provider will deliver to the customer.

Session

In Google Analytics (GA), this is group of actions that take place on a website within a given time frame. Sessions can end for several reasons — for example, leaving the website, X minutes of inactivity, campaign changing. Different platforms will define sessions slightly differently, which needs to be taken into consideration in any review of data. Note for example in GA, sessions also end at midnight with a new session created for the next day, if the user is still active effectively creating two sessions. They are distinct from users.

Session cookies
These are temporary cookies that are erased when your browser is closed. This means that any stored information about browsing or behaviour during that session will be lost if the same website is visited at a later date.

Session ID
Unique number created and stored every time a user visits a webpage or mobile application. It is stored for the duration of that visit.

Sessionisation
The process by which a series of actions or requests to a website are taken and identified as a visit by the same browser. It generally uses some form of session ID, but is handled in different ways by different platforms. *See also Sessions.*

Session replay
Using software to record actual visits to a website and then play them back to see exactly how visitors interacted with the page. Combined with other analytics and testing tools, session replay can provide some really powerful insights.

Sessions to transaction (purchase)
The number of sessions a customer takes before they make a purchase on site. *See also Time to purchase and Days to purchase.*

Seven, plus or minus two
The number of items that can be held in short-term memory or that can be the focus of attention, as stated by George A. Miller in his 1956 paper, "The magic number seven, plus or minus two: Some limits on our capacity for processing information", The Psychological Review, 1956, 63, 81–97 (1956). The number applies only to retention and recall of information, and not to recognition.

SFA (sales force automation)
A type of software that allows all important interactions with a website to be tracked with potential sales prospects and clients including purchases, inventory and order processing.

Shaping
The process of guiding/leading buyers through a series of steps to create a desired response.

Short term (primary/active) memory
The portion of memory that retains a small amount of information in mind in an active, readily available state for a short period of time.

Showrooming
Visiting a physical store in order to examine a product before buying it online at a lower price.

Signal-to-noise ratio (SNR)
The strength of a particular observed effect expressed as a ratio to the background noise associated with measurements of the effect.

Significance and significance level
A measure of determining the validity of an A/B test. It is the probability that a test result is accurate. Also referred to as the alpha value of a test. Usually expressed as a number or percentage (e.g., 0.05 and 5 per cent). Corresponds to the confidence level of test that is in effect 1–alpha per cent. Researchers generally run a test until they have 95 per cent confidence level in the result, so there is only 5 per cent of the result being random. *See also Confidence.*

Silverback app
Usability testing software (Mac-only).

S

Simple inferences

Conclusions drawn from peripheral cues.

Site ID

The company logo needs to be visible throughout a website to reassure visitors that they are where they expect to be.

Site map

A representation of the pages that can be found on a website. It is typically organised in a hierarchical listing. Alternatively, the same information can be represented with boxes and arrows that visually show the hierarchy of the interface.

Site search

This is search activity performed directly on a website and not using external search engines. It can use an internal search engine, navigation menus and tools.

Site speed

How long it takes for a website to load in a browser. The average user now expects a website to load in less than two seconds. In many cases, potential customers will abandon a website if the initial load takes just three seconds. These visitors may not return to the website, citing page load times as the cause.

Situational involvement

When a temporary interest is displayed in a product/service. For example, renting a car or an electrical appliance, staying in a hotel for a holiday, etc.

Sleeper effect

When the source of a message is forgotten but the message itself is still remembered (to varying degrees).

Slot-in answers

In form filling, slot-in answers are those we have in our heads and we don't need external reference sources. *See also Created answers, Gathered answers, and Third-party answers.*

SPA (single page application)

These are web apps that load a single HTML page and dynamically update the content on that page as the user interacts with it, without reloading the page. They can create tracking difficulties for page based analytics systems but this can be resolved with the use of virtual page views, events, etc.

Statistical power

In statistics the formal definition of the power of a test is the probability that it will correctly reject the null hypothesis when the alternative hypothesis is true.

Statistical power is the likelihood that a study will detect an effect when there is an effect to be detected. If statistical power is high, the probability of making a Type II error, or concluding there is no effect when there is one, goes down.

Statistical power is affected chiefly by the size of the effect and the size of the sample used to detect it. Bigger effects are easier to detect than smaller effects, while large samples offer greater test sensitivity than small samples. *See also Type I error, Type II error.*

Status quo

People are reluctant to change their behaviour unless there is a compelling reason to do something different than they'd normally do. Products/services must, therefore, provide sufficient benefits for website visitors to gain added value from buying them, i.e., the value proposition must be convincing and provide sufficient incentive. *See also Value proposition.*

Stock keeping unit (SKU)

The SKU identification code of a product or service can be collected in analytics platforms and reported against as part of performance reviews. *See also Manufacturer part number.*

S

Smarketing

Aligning sales and marketing functions to drive growth. This requires both business functions to work together for common goals.

Smart carts

These remember what's been added to them, whether the customer was logged in or not, or from what device they used to add the item. This saves them a lot of time finding products again and it reduces the number of steps they have to take to continue with their purchase.

Smartphone

Mobile phones with touch screens and often more advanced functionality and options than feature phones.

Social commerce

Using social media to sell.

Social exchange

Negotiated exchanges between different people that help with establishing relationships. It's a cost-benefit scenario with the addition of weighing up alternatives. In the context of websites, to enable social exchange, trust has to be established, reducing anxiety/bad feeling, and increasing rewards — people are more likely to respond if there is a reward.

Social media

Various networking platforms such as Facebook, Twitter, Google Plus, Instagram, YouTube, Pinterest and others. These can be effective for marketing when posting relevant, helpful and informative content that directs people to a website.

Social proof

This refers to how people want to see how others are using and what they think about a product/service. It helps them to appreciate the value the product/service is adding to the lives of existing customers. Importantly, social proof reassures prospective customers that they are making the right decision.

Social relevance

The extent to which something purchased impacts, or is recognised by peers.

Social status

People are concerned whether what they do enhances or diminishes their place in society — whether in their social groups, families, at work, etc. Websites can play to social status by showing visitors well-known people who have bought the product they're interested in and by displaying how many people in general have also bought it. Public forums where customers discuss their products may also help.

Sort

This is a function used on category pages to help website users see available options. These can be presented in a range of useful formats such as most popular, price, size, etc.

Source

A traffic dimension in Google Analytics that identifies the origin of a referral to a website. Generally, it is the name of the website from where the visitor has arrived (or if none it would be "direct") but can also be set manually to identify campaign activity.

Speech recognition

This technology is becoming more commonplace in a variety of technology and most recently in applications like Apple's Siri and Amazon's Alexa. It is useful also as an assistive technology especially to those who have difficulty using their hands. Speech recognition software can also be used to generate closed captioning of conversations which can beneficial for those who are deaf or hard of hearing.

S

Split testing

Alternative phrase that refers to A/B testing and multivariate testing. *See also A/B testing and Multivariate.*

Squeeze page

A type of landing page for capturing opt-in email addresses from potential subscribers.

Staging environment

A parallel implementation for a website or landing page that is used for testing new features or quality assurance before the content is moved to the live or operational environment. A staging environment should be as similar to the live environment as possible.

Stakeholder interviews

Conversations with the key contacts in a business who are responsible for funding, selling, or driving the product.

Stakeholders

All people who have an interest in a website whether internal or external to the business: sales, marketing, customer services, fulfilment, accounts, IT, web design and development, etc.

Stanca Act 2004

In Italy, this Act governs web accessibility requirements for government, private firms (that are licensees of public services), public assistance and rehabilitation agencies, transport and telecoms companies and ICT service contractors. It has 22 technical accessibly requirements in total based on WCAG 2.0 Level A.

Standard error

How much deviation from the average conversion rate can be expected if an experiment is repeated multiple times.

Statistics

The science of collecting, analysing, interpreting and presenting numerical data in large quantities to infer proportions in a whole from those in a representative sample.

Stealth (buzz) marketing

Advertising a product where customers don't realise they are being persuaded to buy something, e.g., people recommending a product on Internet chat forums.

Sticky content

Website content that has been created to keep visitors on the website longer and encourage return visits by customers.

Stimulus

Something that triggers a specific functional reaction.

Stimulus-driven attention

External stimuli that catch someone's attention, for example popups on websites or something that startles is known as stimulus-driven attention. It is a System 1 behaviour and it is also known as "bottom up" attention/behaviour. *See also Bottom up attention and System 1 and System 2.*

Stochastic process

In probability theory, a set of random events drawn from the related underlying distributions. *See also Time series and Event.*

Stock photo

A professionally shot photograph available online for licensing.

Stop words

Words that hinder conversions by triggering a negative psychological reaction.

Story maps

Visualisations that tell a customer's story from their point of view. They are highlighted with icons and colour to show points of brilliance and points of pain.

Storyboard

A tool inspired by the filmmaking industry, where a visual sequence of events is used

S

to capture a user's interactions with a product. Depending on the audience, it may be an extremely rough sketch, purely for crystallising ideas.

Storytelling

Asking buyers to recount their own personal stories about buying, using and/or disposing of a product/service. This provides insights into their needs and identifies the product/service attributes that meet them. Also, people tend to remember stories. Therefore, websites can include stories — testimonials, case studies, reviews, endorsements — about the products/services they sell to help visitors remember what they've seen. This assists with telling the story to others.

Strategy stage

The brand, guiding principles, and long-term vision of an organisation are articulated at this stage. The strategy will shape the goals of the project — what the organisation is hoping to achieve with the project, how its success should be measured, and what priority it should have in the grand scheme of things.

Strong argument

The best or central attributes of a product/service presented convincingly.

Stroop effect

A demonstration to highlight interference in the reaction times of a task. It is often used to highlight the conflict between our dual processing brain (Systems 1 and 2). For example, name the colour of the words, but do not read the words.

SEE FIGURE 24

Subhead

A small heading within the main body of longer copy. These can help with scanability by breaking the copy up into smaller chunks. *See also Scanability.*

Subjective comprehension

What someone thinks they have knowledge of something/understand what it is about, regardless of the accuracy of the information.

Subjective norms

Perceived social pressure to engage or not to engage in a particular behaviour.

Subliminal perception

Activation of sensory receptors by stimuli outside of our conscious perception.

Substantiation

Supporting evidence for claims made about a product/service.

Success metrics

Specific numbers hoped to be improved by a test. Defining the success of an A/B test involves understanding and defining the success metrics.

Summative (conclusion) research

Done at the end of a project to determine its success.

Sunk cost effect

This occurs when people continue with an activity although it fails their expectations. They continue simply because they have invested time/money (or both) in the activity.

Supporting arguments

Details such as pros and cons that agree with and strengthen the marketing message.

Surprise and delight

A marketing and customer engagement tactic that is used to catch customers off guard (surprising them) in a positive fashion (delighting them). For example, a common tactic is randomly selecting a sample or individual customer to receive a free gift or experience.It can also be used to positively engage with customers in unexpected ways — e.g., handwritten

S

personal thankyou notes in order deliveries. This can create customer loyalty and brand advocacy.

Survey
An online form designed to solicit feedback from current or potential customers.

Surveying
Surveying people while they are on a website, or after they have recently visited a website, can provide useful qualitative data, providing researchers have set appropriate, relevant questions. The sample needs to be within the range of 100 to 200 people to get a balanced view of the audience — small samples can skew the results because in smaller groups, the louder voices get heard above the others! It's important that the questions asked will provide information that can be used to improve a website and its offering(s).

S

Switches
Switches are used by many people with severe physical or cognitive impairment and allow these users to operate computers. They come in a variety of shapes and sizes each of which depends on the action that the user has to take to activate them (sip-puff, pushing, pulling, pressing, blinking or squeezing).

Symbolic innovation

Products/services/attributes/ideas that gain new social meaning.

Symbolic needs
These relate to how people see themselves and how others perceive them, how they relate to them and what they think of them.

Symbolic self-completion theory
When people believe that they are incomplete and, therefore, try to change the way they see themselves by acquiring and displaying symbols.

Symbols
Those things that people use for expressing and supporting their identity.

Synapse
The gap and junction between one neuron and another. One neuron releases a neurotransmitter, which binds with the another, passing an electrochemical message on the neural pathway.

Syncratic decision
Where people make a joint decision.

System 1 and System 2
A theory that the brain operates using two processes consisting of an implicit (automatic), unconscious process, System 1, and an explicit (controlled), conscious process, System 2.

Daniel Kahneman, noble prize winner and author of *"Thinking, Fast and Slow"* describes System 1 as fast, instinctive and emotional, while System 2 is slower, deliberative and logical. It's the System 2 mode that marketers are concerned with, encouraging us to think about our purchasing.

Endless Gain has published a guide book titled *"Selling Fast and Slow: How understanding the brain's two systems can boost your sales"*. Download your own electronic copy of the guide book from the Amazon Kindle bookstore.

SEE FIGURE 25

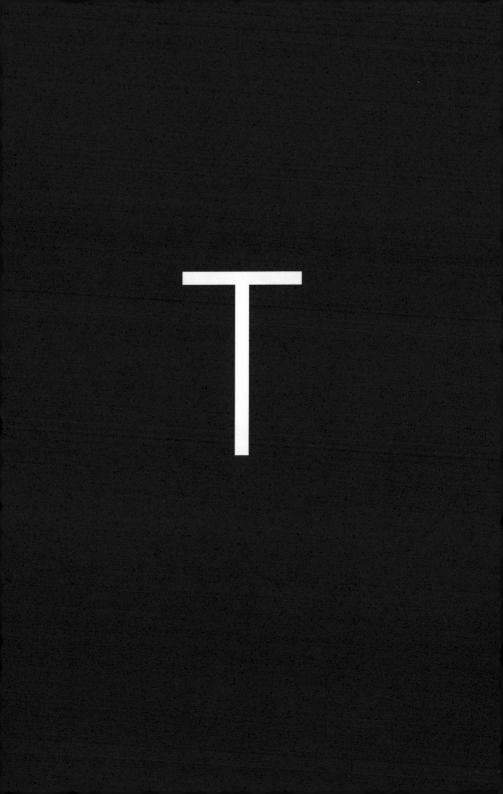

Tab key navigation test.

This test will confirm whether or not items on a webpage are keyboard operable. Often used in manual accessibility testing and in combination with a "select all" test.

Tag line/tagline

A memorable short phrase that tells website visitors exactly what a website is all about. For example, Endless Gain's tagline is: By applying data and psychology, we will convert more of your online visitors into customers.

Tag/tags manager

Tags are metadata inserted in webpages. Using a tag management tool enables easier management of tags without having to understand code or have to rely on IT departments to do the work.

Taguchi method

A specific type of fractional factorial design of experiments (DOE) approach commonly used in manufacturing optimisation and sometimes applied to landing page optimisation. *See also Fractional factorial and Design of experiments.*

Target findability

An eye tracking measure of how long it takes a website visitor to find a link or a button — i.e. the target.

Target recognition

When a website visitor finds a target they will fixate on it. They then have to understand its purpose and use it. The time it takes from finding the target to recognising what it can do and then using it can be measured with eye tracking technology.

Task

A procedure that includes goals, steps, skills, start state, inputs, end state, and outputs to accomplish an activity.

Task analysis

A method used to identify and understand the activities to be performed by users when interacting with a website.

Taxonomy

A scheme for classifying a body of knowledge and defining the relationships among the pieces. Sometimes referred to as a controlled vocabulary, a taxonomy is often used to classify content to aid in the creation of information architecture. *See also Information architecture.*

Technical communication

Easily accessible technical/specialised information for a specific audience.

Technical writing

This is business of writing technical documentation aimed at helping people to use a product or service — whether it is something being sold or to assist them with using a website.

Temporal lobe

The human brain has a left and right temporal lobe. The left deals with the right side of the body, while the right deals with the left side of the body. They are found in the ventral region of the lateral part of the cortex. They play an important role in organising sensory input, auditory perception, language and speech production, as well as memory association and formation.

Terminal value

A desirable end state, for example pleasure, recognition, etc.

Test duration

Refers to how long a test should run for. Determining the duration of the test requires consideration of expected uplift from the variations over the control, numbers of unique visitors included in the test, number of variations to be tested, and the level of confidence needed. Things to

T

consider include, the expected uplift over the control, unique visitors on the test, number of alternative variations and how confident in the answer is needed. As a starting point tests should be run for full weeks (not part weeks) and they should run for a minimum of two business cycles.

Testimonials

Quotes from customers that help and in some cases cause damage (negative testimonial) to a brand.

Testing

Critical evaluation of something, for example, a specific webpage or element on a webpage, to discover how well it works. This is an extremely important part of conversion optimisation that eliminates guessing. Without testing it would not be possible to validate hypotheses and see whether they work and provide real improvements. *See also A/B testing.*

Testing platforms

Software that allows tests to be run on a website.

Test protocol

A test protocol details the activities and steps taken to test a particular set of features on a website.

Thalamus

The thalamus connects areas of the cerebral cortex that are involved in sensory perception and movement with other parts of the central nervous system.

Theory of reasoned action

An explanation of how, when, and why attitudes predict buyer behaviour.

Think-aloud protocol

A direct observation method of user testing that involves asking participants to think out loud as they are performing a task. Participants are asked to say whatever they are looking at, thinking, doing, and feeling

at each moment. This method is especially helpful for determining their expectations and identifying what aspects of a system are confusing.

Third-party answers

In form filling, it may be necessary to ask other people to supply information. *See also Created answers, Gathered answers and Slot-in answers.*

Third-party cookie

Cookies set by a domain or website that is different to the one the user is currently visiting. Often used by advertisers and tracking technologies. *See also Cookies.*

Three click rule

This is an unofficial web design rule concerning the design of website navigation. It suggests that a website visitor should be able to find any information with no more than three mouse clicks. It is based on the belief that they will get frustrated and often leave if they cannot find the information within the three clicks. However, it's not necessarily the number of clicks needed to complete an action that is important; it's the ease of making the clicks that needs considering when designing the pathway through a website. Five easy clicks can be better than three mental energy-sapping clicks.

Throttling

Restricting the percentage of available traffic that is allocated to certain test recipes or restricting the percentage of traffic allocated to the test in general is known as throttling.

Thumbnail image

Small product images usually seen on the category (product listing) pages and next to the main hero image on the product pages of ecommerce sites.

T

Time lag

A Google Analytics report that counts the number of days from the first user interaction (e.g., impression, click, direct session) to conversion.

Time metrics

Time-based metrics are a series of metrics that quantify the amount of time spent on something. For example, time on page, time on site, and session duration.

Time risk

The uncertainty felt by a customer about how long it will take to buy a product/service. It can also involve how much time it takes to use the product/service and/or dispose of it.

Time series

A stochastic process with time-based sampling. *See also Stochastic process.*

Time to first fixation

The amount of time that it takes a person to look at a specific AOI on a webpage or app. This can be measured with eye tracking. By understanding the time to fixation within webpage design, the data can be used to inform the testing to make the customer experience better. *See also Eye tracking.*

SEE FIGURE 13

Time to purchase

The length of time it takes consumers to make the decision to purchase (or another conversion type). Frequently used as a measure of the sales cycle of a website/product. This information is important in understanding how users are visiting a website at different times and ways as part of their customer journey. In Google Analytics ecommerce reporting, this is distinguished between the number of days to transaction and the number of sessions to transaction.

Title tag

This defines the title of a webpage. The title will be displayed above the meta description in search engine results pages.

Tone

The personality of a website sets the tone for the interaction (conversation) with the visitors to the site.

Tool tip

Usually a smaller box with information that appears or pops up if a user puts their mouse over a designated graphical or text element. *See also Hover help.*

Top down attention

Looking at something voluntarily based on a prior knowledge or current goal.

Trace strength

The strength of linkages between an association and a concept in our memory.

Trackback

When other websites reference another website, Google Analytics' trackback feature notifies the webmaster.

Trackball

An assistive technology that acts as a pointing device. It consists of a ball which is held into place by a socket that contains sensors to detect the rotation of the ball. Trackballs offer a number of advantages over mouse input because they have a limitless scroll plane, are easier to manipulate with fingers and thumbs, and allow integrated buttons to be activated without affecting pointer position.

Tracking

Tracking is the space between letters. When we track bodies of text, we are adjusting space between every letter in a sentence in order to change the density or appearance of a large block of type (i.e., in body copy), with the goal of improving legibility.

Tracking code

HTML code inserted into a website that enables Google Analytics to collect data from it.

Traffic

The visitors coming to a website from various sources. It is the digital equivalent to footfall in physical bricks and mortar stores. Analysing website traffic helps to understand how slowly or how quickly visitors convert.

Trailing off

A technique used in moderated user testing, whereby the moderator asks part of a question, and trails off, rather than asking a complete thorough question. This encourages the participant to act or fill in the gaps. For example; User – *"Will clicking here add it to my basket?"*, Moderator – *"Hmmm, you're wondering if … (pause) ?"*. See also Columbo technique and Moderated user testing.

Transduction

The action or process of converting something and especially energy or a message into another form.

Transformational advertising

This is an approach aimed at increasing emotional involvement with a product or a service.

Transformational culture (and leadership)

The process or approach to dynamically changing the culture of an organisation so that it can adapt to internal and external forces. Often mentioned as an approach required to fully embrace a testing culture within an organisation.

Treatment

Test pages used in conversion optimisation research are known as treatments. They contain variables — the element(s) that is(are) being tested, such as a headline, image, layout, copy, a button, and so on — and values — specific versions of the variables being tested. So, the values represent the different versions of the new headline, etc. Therefore, treatments display the new values for the variable being tested.

Trialability

The length of time limited to trying a product/service before it is bought.

Triggers

Used to encourage a consumer to act. They are often positioned next to CTA buttons. Free delivery, Last two remaining, 10-year guarantee, etc., are examples.

Triggers can be classified as both "hot" and "cold".

For example, something that a user can do immediately is a hot trigger — i.e., CTA buttons to "Get immediate access" or "Download now". Whereas, high street adverts for websites that people see while driving/walking by are cold triggers.

Triune brain

Theory by Paul D. Maclean states that our brain has three parts — reptilian (survival instincts), mammalian (emotions, connections, rewards) and neocortex (thinking, planning, deciding). Although it is still referred to when trying to explain buying behaviour by some marketing specialists, the theory is contested by modern science. *See also Reptilian brain, Limbic system and Neocortex.*

Trust

Something that must be earned from website visitors/customers. Use consistent messages and design, testimonials, guarantees, trust seals and badges, provide great service and support, etc.

T

Trust badges

Logos and seals displayed on a website to help signify the safety and security of a website. *See also Trust.*

Truth effect

When we believe something just because it has been repeated continually.

T-test

A t-test is a statistical analyses of the means of two populations. It generally uses small sample sizes to test the difference between the samples when the variances of two normal distributions are unknown. In other words, a t-test determines a probability that two populations are the same with respect to the variable tested.

Tweet

A tweet is a post made on the social media network Twitter.

Twitter

Twitter is a free microblogging platform that allows users to broadcast short posts called tweets.

Two column forms

Avoid using two column forms as they can be confusing. Scanning from one column to another requires much more effort and causes friction.

Two-sided message

Marketing that provides positive and negative information.

Two-tailed test (two-sided test)

A two-tailed test is testing for the possibility of a relationship in either direction compared to the normal distribution of the original sample. It tests against the possibility that the treatment could either be better or perform worse than the control.

Type I error

The incorrect rejection of a true null hypothesis (false positive). Essentially detecting an effect that is not present.

SEE FIGURE 26

Type II error

The incorrect rejection of a true alternative hypothesis retaining a false null hypothesis (false negative). Failing to detect an effect that is present.

SEE FIGURE 26

Typography

The artistic arrangement of type in a readable and visually appealing way. Typography usually concerns the design and use of various typefaces in a way that helps to better visually communicate ideas. But be careful when using typographic variations — bold, italic, all capitals, underlining, superscript, subscript, etc. — to prevent confusion. *See also Legibility.*

T

UAAG 2.0

Currently in draft form, these guidelines from the World Wide Web Consortium (WC3) are aimed at the developers of web browsers, browser extensions and media players. They are useful also for assistive technology developers to allow them to understand the types of accessible information to expect from UAAG 2.0 compliant user agents. They are structured in a similar way to WCAG 2.0 and have the same levels of conformance, level A, AA or AAA.

Underlining

People tend to think that underlined words indicate a hyperlink. So, think about the context before using underlining. And, try to avoid doing it to prevent confusion and frustration. *See also Legibility, Readability and Typography.*

Unique selling proposition(s)

Also known as a USP or USPs, these make up the basis of effective marketing. A USP can be described as what differentiates a product or service from its competitors. Careful definition of a USP is necessary but can be achieved with good research, such as establishing what motivates consumer behaviour and buying decisions and discovering the reasons customers ultimately buy a product over a competitor's offering.

Uniques

Shorthand for unique users to a website over a period of time. Sometimes also used to describe any metrics that are defined as unique providing that the same item is not counted multiple times within a given time frame. For example, unique users, unique visits, and unique page views.

Unique visitors

These are the individual people who visit a website during a specific period of time. When measuring the total number of unique visitors, do not count repeat visits by the same person. Often used interchangeably with unique users (though not to be confused with visits and sessions).

Unmoderated user testing

In this type of user test there is no moderator to oversee the participant(s). They complete specific, pre-defined tasks by themselves. Their own computer, tablet or smartphone records their on-screen actions and their comments. It is possible to gain valuable insights from unmoderated user tests but there are some disadvantages when compared to moderated sessions. *See also Moderated user testing and Remote user testing.*

Unnoticeable difference

The subconscious pays more attention to something very slightly different from what is normally expected to be seen.

Up-selling

Selling an existing customer or potential customer an upgraded version of the product/service on offer.

Urgency

Creating a sense of urgency is a persuasive technique used to encourage visitors to act quickly to a call to action. Stating deadlines, such as a special time-limited offer, or using scarcity to highlight low numbers of products, for example, can help encourage the visitor to take fast action.

URL (uniform resource locator)

Every webpage has a URL that is used to identify the page and the server on which the page resides.

Usability

Usability is much more than ensuring everything on a website works across all browsers/devices. It requires a thorough understanding of how quickly and easily visitors are able to make use of the website. And, because of the

U

nonexistence of an average website visitor/customer, usability needs to be universal to allow everyone to use it.

Usability engineering

Improving the usability of a product by assessing and making recommendations.

Usability lab

A facility where usability testing is done giving the ability to capture and analyse human behaviour when interacting with technological devices (computers, mobiles, games, etc.).

Use innovativeness

When a product is used for something other than it was originally intended.

User-centred design

A design process during which the needs of the user is considered at all times. Designers consider how a user is likely to use the product, and they then test the validity of their assumptions in real world tests with actual users.

User feedback loop

Ideas are put in front of website users so that they can provide feedback. This is used to refine the design, and then the process is repeated.

User friendly

Refers to how easy something is to learn/ operate. However, concluding a webpage is user friendly should be based on testing, not on the opinions of people running the website.

User-generated (user-created) content

Content such as blog comments, tweets, questions on forums and reviews, or any form of media that is produced by the users of a website or online service.

User ID

A unique persistent string ID to represent a single user in Google Analytics. This can be persistent for signed in users making it possible to track a single user across different devices when signed in. Note this should be non-personally identifiable.

User intent

What a user's intentions are and how likely they are to achieve them (to convert).

User interview

Used for understanding the tasks and motivations of the user group for whom a website is designed. User interviews may be formally scheduled, or just informal chats.

User journey

The step-by-step journey that a user takes to reach their goal.

User research

Observation techniques, task analyses, and other feedback methodologies that focus on understanding user behaviours, needs, and motivations.

User test

A user sits in front of a website or app and performs tasks and thinks out loud while doing so. It is important to ensure test participants are appropriately screened to represent the type of audience expected to use the website being tested.

User testing

Testing websites on real people. Websites can be tested in real-time in a lab-based experiment, which can provide a quick route to identifying problems and fixing them. User testing can help with answering important questions such as:

- Why are people bouncing from the website?
- Why are a lot of visitors being lost on category pages?

U

- Why does the search function not convert as expected?
- Why are customers not proceeding to the checkout?
- Why are customers dropping out of the checkout?

It will show why something doesn't work, how the visitor would like to use the website, and what causes friction. Importantly, it allows treatments to be tested across all browsers and devices with real website users without having to make the treatments live on the website. *See also Moderated user testing, Remote user testing and Unmoderated user testing.*

Users
A metric in analytics to identify unique individuals over a period of time across multiple visits to a website potentially via multiple devices. In comparison to sessions that are for specific visits only.

Utility theory
The way in which we make decisions, based upon rational and an optimal choice behaviour.

UX (user experience)
"The first requirement for an exemplary user experience is to meet the exact needs of the customer, without fuss or bother. Next comes simplicity and elegance that produce products that are a joy to own, a joy to use." (D Norman and J Nielsen, Nielsen Norman Group.) UX is complex. It covers *"Every aspect of the user's interaction with a product, service, or company that make up the user's perceptions of the whole. User experience design as a discipline is concerned with all the elements that together make up that interface, including layout, visual design, text, brand, sound, and interaction. UX works to coordinate these elements to allow for the best possible interaction by users."* - *User Experience Professionals Association.*

UXPin
Collaborative app that includes stencils for wireframing and low-fidelity prototyping.

U

Valence
Intrinsic attractiveness (positive valence) or aversiveness (negative valence) of a product/service. Also used to describe specific emotions.

Validity
The extent to which data and results reflect the real world. Validity covers the concepts/hypotheses under investigation, the sample of the population being studied, the data collection methods, and the outcomes (results/findings) of the experiments/research.

Validity threats
Test results may look conclusive when they aren't conclusive. Therefore, there is a need for awareness of what may threaten the validity of tests in addition to sample size. These validity threats are known as effects and include:

- History effect — this occurs when external factors interfere with your tests and challenge their validity. For example, marketing campaigns, holiday seasons — Christmas, Easter, etc., the various seasons themselves, good/bad PR, product recalls and so on.
- Instrumentation effect — this is caused by issues with the testing tools (or instruments) that result in flawed test data. For example, inserting incorrect tracking on a website. This is a common error that harms results.
- Selection effect — this results from incorrectly assuming a segment of the traffic accurately represents the total. For example, it can occur when promotion acquired traffic hits your website, skewing the results.
- Broken code effect — this is caused by unknown bugs in a test that produce flawed data. For example, these bugs might mean that the variation isn't displaying correctly on some browsers and devices.

Value
People assign specific values to a variable in a landing page test. When several distinct values are assigned to a variable, it is known as a branching factor.

A person's judgement about what they believe to be good, bad, important, etc.

Value added by marketing
Value added by marketing is computed by subtracting the market value of purchased goods from the market value of goods sold.

Value based pricing
A price setting process based on the value the product provides to the customer.

Value exchange
Exchanging something of value for website visitors' contact details which are of high value. So a sale or subscription can be classed as a value exchange. A value exchange can also be exchanging downloadable content in return for contact information.

Value proposition
A clear statement that describes why a prospective customer should buy a product or service. It will describe its uniqueness and its relevance to the customer and why it will provide them with a better solution than those offered by other brands.

Value segmentation
Grouping buyers by common values.

Value system
Sets of values categorised by importance.

Values and life style survey
A psychographic tool to gather and measure variable demographic, value, attitude, and lifestyle information. *See also Psychographics.*

Vanity metrics

Vanity metrics are things like free downloads, clicks on blog posts, and raw page views. They do not necessarily correlate to the numbers that really matter: sales, revenues and profits. The latter are more actionable metrics.

Variable

A variable is specific landing page tuning element or page section in a landing page test. It's called a "factor" in statistical testing.

Variable interactions

This phenomenon occurs when the setting for one variable in a test influences the setting of another variable either positively or negatively. The majority of fractional factorial approaches assume that there are no variable interactions, however, many landing page tests show very strong variable interactions. *See also Positive interactions, and Negative interactions.*

Variance

During a statistical experiment, the variance is the square of the sample noise. Bigger samples have less noise, so the variance decreases. To work out the standard deviation, work out the square root of the variance.

Variation

A version of a webpage that differs from the original or baseline. The variation or variations are tested against the original.

Vicarious exploration

Seeking information simply for stimulation. Going through catalogues, searching websites, etc.

Views

In Google Analytics (GA), this can refer to reporting views that are the level at which the data is viewed for a given analytics property (where property refers to the specific GA code implemented on a website). Within GA accounts there can be multiple views for a property to which it is possible to apply different filters or actions to create subsets of the original data. For example, filtering out traffic to the website from development teams or having a view for only a specific geographic location. GA automatically creates an unfiltered view when creating a property and it is best practice to maintain this to allow webmasters to see the raw collected data at any time. (Also shorthand for metrics such as page views.)

Vimeo

Vimeo is a video-sharing website where users can upload, share and view videos.

Viral marketing

Consumer-to-consumer communication that supports a particular offering which spreads widely and quickly over the Internet via social media.

Virtuous data quality cycle

A description of the chain of actions that reinforce themselves with positive results in a feedback loop. Used for the process in a data quality program in which continuous analysis, observation and improvement is cyclical feeding into positive outcomes in ongoing data management. Also can be applied to business intelligence.

Vision

The ability to see by detecting wavelengths of light and processing them. Vision is the most important sense for the majority of people and what they see will result in them taking action or trigger their thinking.

Visits

Alternative term for an analytics metric that is generally an equivalent to sessions.

Visitors

Alternative term for "user" in analytics.

V

Visual cortex

The part of the cerebral cortex that processes visual information, allowing people to see and understand what they see.

Visual (communication) design

Combining design and information development in order to communicate a media message to a target audience.

Visual cueing

This is a technique for directing attention. Arrows, for example, can be used to emphasise the most important content on a webpage. Visual cues can also be used to distract attention away from less favourable or less important content.

Visual fluency

How easily a person processes visual stimuli, i.e., how easily they make sense of what they see.

Visual hierarchy

The arrangement or presentation of elements in a way that implies importance. It influences the order in which the human eye perceives what it sees.

Visual noise

Anything that does not contribute directly to the user experience for website visitors.

Visual sensory path

People begin processing what they see in the eye's retina. This is where photoreceptors — rod and cone cells — connect to ganglion cells in the optic nerves. The information is transmitted by these to the brain through the optic nerves (one for each eye) to reach the lateral geniculate body and onto the occipital lobes in the brain for further processing to enable a person to make sense of what they see. *See also Eye.*

Visualisation (data from tests)

Visualisations can represent an individual or aggregate data collected from a group. They can be static or dynamic. These can be presented as both spatial and temporal data, dependent on the test's requirements.

Vocabulary checker

Useful to verify that familiar words are being used. Example checkers include: The Longman Vocabulary Checker, SpellCheckPlus, and Sentencechecker. *See also Jargon.*

Voice of the customer (VOC)

Feedback direct from customers, which can be collected in person, from a survey, from a focus group, or through observation. *See also Ethnography/ Ethnographic research.*

Voice of the employee (VOE)

Feedback from front-line employees who deal with customers every day. Collect the data in person, by shadowing front-line staff, or by interviewing or surveying them.

Voice of the institution (VOI)

Feedback from senior strategic stakeholders who have a good overall understanding of a business and what may be affecting the customer experience for better or worse. Collect the data using one-on-one interviews or by surveys.

Von Restorff effect (isolation effect)

Automatically paying more attention to things that are significantly different. The effect was discovered by and named after the psychologist Hedwig von Restorff.

W

W3C (World Wide Web Consortium)

An international community of member organisations, W3C staff, and the public working together to develop web standards.

WAI-ARIA

Web Accessibility Initiative-Accessible Rich Internet Applications (WAI-ARIA) is a technical specification published by the World Wide Web Consortium (W3C) that defines specific roles, states and properties for custom interactions that assistive technology is able to understand in a web environment to optimise accessibility.

Walkthroughs

Replicating the customer journey through a website using every relevant device and browser. The idea is to go through the whole shopping process while being aware of bugs and user experience problems and recording them. The researcher will do everything that a customer is expected to do, for example fill out forms, click all the buttons and links, etc. *See also User testing and Usability.*

Warranty

A written guarantee issued to customers that the product/service they have bought is fit for purpose and that there is a promise to repair or replace it if necessary within a specified period of time. Displaying a warranty statement could help reduce friction.

Waterfall model of software development

A sequential design process. Progress flows steadily through Conception > Initiation > Analysis > Design > Construction > Testing > Implementation > Maintenance.

Watermarking

A method of marking a photograph/ document with the owner's identity and preventing image/information theft.

WCAG 2.0

The WCAG are a set of guidelines produced by the World Wide Web Consortium (W3C) to help develop websites so that they are accessible to people with disabilities. It has four guiding principles in that website content must be Perceivable, Operable, Understandable and Robust (POUR). Websites should aim to reach one of three conformance levels to WCAG; Level A, AA or AAA. The level of conformance required may be determined by legal requirements of a particular country, but Level AA is generally the agreed level of compliance websites should endeavour to meet.

Wear out

Inattention and possible irritation that occurs after an audience or target market has encountered a specific advertisement/promotion too many times. *See also Adaptation.*

Web analytics

The measurement, collection, analysis and reporting of web data so that it is possible to understand usage and optimise webpages. Software can be used for analysing and tracking the behaviour of visitors on a website.

Web and exit surveys

These usually take the format of pop-up questionnaires that appear to website visitors at strategic points during their visit. For example, after a certain time, after visiting a certain number of webpages, after a particular activity, etc. *See also Surveys.*

Web forms

A web form allows a website visitor to enter purchasing/subscription/enquiry/service data that is sent to a server for processing. They fill in the forms using checkboxes, buttons, or text fields. Forms can cause friction if they are perceived complicated or intrusive, requiring more data than the visitor is prepared to give or difficult questions that need information that the visitor may not have at hand. It is advisable to test forms before they are made live on a website. *See also Forms.*

Web personalisation

How website content changes based on user activity or location. It is a data-driven approach that gives consumers a personalised experience accounting for their buying habits, the type of products they search for and buy, and attempts to answer their needs on an individual level. *See also Personalisation.*

Web traffic surveys

A survey run on a website to collect direct feedback from visitors. They can be advantageous in obtaining feedback from visitors who are otherwise anonymous. Such surveys are, therefore, a useful research tool for helping understand why they visited the website — what are they looking for, what problem are they experiencing etc.

Weber's law

Helps with understanding consumer behaviour and guiding a marketing strategy. For example, it helps to focus on how different something must be before customers notice the difference and are prepared to pay for it. It is more concerned with proportions rather than actual numbers. For example, if someone wants to buy a new tablet PC they may think the percentage difference in price between the basic specific/configuration and the next one up doesn't warrant the additional money spending on it and so they'll stick with the lower spec product. But, if buying a car, a similar amount for upgrading the entertainment system wouldn't be an issue as the percentage difference is lower.

Webmaster

The person who looks after a website.

Webmaster tools

A set of tools for webmasters to check a website status and optimise visibility in search engines. Generally thought of with regards to Google, but other search engines, such as Bing, have their own tools for their own results. Commonly still used to refer to the Google platform although this has now been renamed the "Google Search Console".

Welcome email

An automated email response to new customers/subscribers. It also gives an opportunity to ask customers to link to social media platforms.

Wheel of Consumer Analysis

Wheel of Consumer Analysis (JP Peter and JC Olson) is a framework to help marketers understand consumer behaviour in order to design their marketing strategy.

The wheel keeps turning in response to changes in consumers and in marketing strategy. The hub of the wheel is the marketing strategy. Consumer affect refers to consumers' feelings such as whether they like or dislike a product. Cognition is how they think about a particular product. Behaviour are the actions of consumers that can be directly observed and measured. The consumer environment is everything external to consumers that influences what they think, feel, and do; for example, what others say, advertising, etc.

White space

Also called negative space, white space refers to the areas of a design that are not filled with content. White space is an important design element as it helps to let a design "breathe", helps avoid overly complicated designs, and keeps designs looking clean. It also helps clarity within a website. *See also Clarity.*

Whitelist

Whitelists are used frequently with email applications to allow users to compile lists of senders they wish to receive email from. For them, it prevents being spammed, with the unwanted email being consigned to a junk email folder. As an online business, a domain should be whitelisted by customers to prevent messages being filtered. This can be done by encouraging customers to physically add the domain to their whitelist and when running mass email campaigns, use a third party commercial whitelist that has arrangements with ISPs to allow email to pass their filtering systems.

Widget

A live update on a website, webpage, desktop or mobile device. Widgets contain personalised, neatly organised content or applications selected by the user.

WIIFM

"What's in it for me" should be at the forefront of the mind when thinking like customers, particularly when it comes to producing website content and marketing communications.

Willingness to recommend

A metric related to customer satisfaction. When a customer is satisfied with a product, he or she might recommend it to friends, relatives and colleagues.

Wireframe

A rough guide for the layout of a website or app, either done with pen and paper or with wireframing software.

Within-page links

Within-page links are used on pages that contain several (e.g., three or more) screenfuls of information. Within-page links are best arranged as a table of contents for the page. Within-page links allow users to skip through textual information, resulting in a more efficient information-finding process. *See also Anchor links.*

Wizard of Oz

A user-based evaluation of unimplemented technology where, generally unknown to the user, a human or team is simulating some or all the responses of the system. *See also Usability.*

Word of mouth

Communication with and between friends, family, and peers.

Workflow diagram

A graphical representation of activities and actions conducted by users of a system. (Sometimes called an activity diagram.)

Wow factor

The instant appeal of a product that impresses and surprises people the first time they see it.

WYSIATI

"What you see is all there is"; after Daniel Khaneman from his book "Thinking, fast and slow". When the mind makes decisions, it deals mainly with "known knowns", phenomena it has already observed. It rarely considers "known unknowns", phenomena that it knows to be relevant but about which it has no information. Finally, it appears oblivious to the possibility of "unknown unknowns", unknown phenomena of unknown relevance.

WYSIWYG

An acronym for "what you see is what you get". It describes the way in which the layout on the graphical screen represents a printed version of a document.

X

X-browser and device testing

Cross-browser testing. It is essential that websites function properly using all browsers and across all devices. *See also Walkthroughs.*

X-device tracking and user behaviour

Cross-device tracking. This is how website customers are identified across smartphones, tablets and desktop computers. Bear in mind consumers might use multiple devices to shop with, for example, they may start with a smartphone and then switch to a tablet or a laptop to complete their tasks. *Criteo, reckons, "Cross-device usage is now enormous. Cross-device purchasing powers 45 per cent of ecommerce transactions".*

X-height

The average height of lowercase letters. X-height gets its name as this value is usually exemplified by looking at the height of the letter x in any given typeface. A typeface with a small x-height can prove challenging to read at a lower point size and therefore it is important to consider x-height when selecting a font for body copy.

XML feeds

Paid inclusion in which a search engine is fed information about an advertiser's webpages via XML, rather than requiring that the engine gather that information through crawling actual pages. Marketers pay to have their pages included in a spider-based search index based on an XML format document that represents each page on the advertiser website. Advertisers pay either annually per URL or on a CPC basis — and are assured of frequent crawl cycles. New media types are being introduced into paid inclusion, including graphics, video, audio, and rich media.

Y

Yahoo!

One of the first web directories that expanded into search and other services. It's the third most popular search engine, with Google the top, then Bing. Yahoo! Search is powered by Microsoft's Bing search engine.

Yammer

Yammer is a freemium enterprise social networking service used for private communication within organisations.

Yerkes-Dodson law

This describes how performance in a task varies with arousal. As a person's arousal increases, so does their performance — but only to a point — after which increasing arousal decreases performance. Because of this, a person may select the first thing that will reduce that arousal, even if it is a less than satisfactory solution. *See also Satisficing.*

You are not your user

A reminder of the importance of customer research and that assumptions around user behaviour are lazy and unhelpful.

YouTube

A global video-sharing platform owned by Google. YouTube has more than a billion users, 80 per cent of which are outside of the USA.